SHOULD
You
ADOPT?

Also by Christine Moriarty Field

Coming Home to Raise Your Children

SHOULD *You* ADOPT?

CHRISTINE MORIARTY FIELD

Fleming H. Revell
A Division of Baker Book House Co
Grand Rapids, Michigan 49516

© 1997 by Christine M. Field

Published by Fleming H. Revell
a division of Baker Book House Company
P.O. Box 6287, Grand Rapids, MI 49516-6287

Printed in the United States of America

Library of Congress Cataloging-in-Publication Data

Field, Christine M., 1956–
   Should you adopt? / Christine Moriarty Field.
         p.   cm.
      ISBN 0-8007-5628-2 (paper)
      1. Adoption. 2. Adopted children. 3. Adoptive parents. I. Title.
   HV875.F54   1997
   362.73'4—dc21   97-3213

Unless otherwise indicated, Scripture quotations are taken from the HOLY BIBLE, NEW INTERNATIONAL VERSION®. NIV®. Copyright © 1973, 1978, 1984 by International Bible Society. Used by permission of Zondervan Publishing House. All rights reserved.

For current information about all releases from Baker Book House, visit our web site:

http://www.bakerbooks.com

Contents

Preface

I
Did not plant you.
True.
But when
The season is done—
When the alternate
Prayers for sun
And for rain
Are counted—
When the pain
Of weeding
And the pride of
Watching are through—
Then I will hold you
High to heaven.
A shining sheaf
Above the thousand
Seeds grown wild.

Not my planting.
But by heaven,
My harvest—
My child.

                    Anonymous

This book is lovingly dedicated to my family. My husband, Mark, has been my constant supporter, my dream-sharer, and my best friend. My children, Clare, Caitlin, and Grace, are gifts of God who made this story possible.

This book is for information and encouragement and is not intended to be a substitute for competent legal counsel. No attorney-client relationship is formed between the author or publisher and the purchaser or reader of this book. Although reasonable efforts have been made to ensure the accuracy of the information, the author and the publisher assume no responsibility for errors or omissions herein. The author and the publisher further disclaim any liability for injury suffered because of information provided herein. Please consult closely with your adoption attorney regarding the specific issues and procedures involved in your adoptive situation.

Laws vary from state to state and each adoption is unique. Statutory and case law may change abruptly and are always subject to judicial interpretation. While this book discusses many legal issues, my intent is to give you a glimpse of the adoptive process and to share the joy of being an adoptive family. May God bless you on your journey.

 # ONE

Waiting for Grace

never planned on motherhood. My career as a lawyer was challenging and satisfying. The desire for children crept up on me silently but surely around age thirty. We were happily married and enjoying the benefits of being DINKs—Double Incomes, No Kids.

Wham! Baby fever hit forcefully with the persistent ticking of my biological clock. And so we embarked on our journey to become a family. We thought it was good that we had waited because we were really emotionally ready to be parents.

But then, after we decided to have a baby, we waited. And waited. And waited. About a year into this process, we began to explore infertility issues and take some preliminary tests. We also started to contact domestic adoption agencies but were disheartened to learn of the five- to seven-year wait for a healthy, white infant. As time went on with no baby in our family portrait, we began the application process for adoption with a private agency. We also told everyone we knew, like doctor friends and other lawyers, that we were interested in adoption. Then we turned the whole process over to God and trusted him to work it out as he saw fit. We left that summer for a vacation in Ireland, not realizing that this would be our last trip as DINKs.

9

On our return home, we were amazed to learn that I was pregnant. I had been pregnant for six to eight weeks.

Thermometers and fertility charts were no strangers to us. Although we hadn't taken heroic measures to become pregnant, we were pretty serious about the project. I remember purchasing a handheld computer/thermometer device called "The Rabbit," which would store all of our fertility data and help calculate days of maximum fertility. When the device arrived, I concluded that it was a little too mechanistic for me and returned it to the manufacturer.

We had been through so many pregnancy tests that we had a little ritual. We would make a conference call and both of us would wait on the phone for the results. This time was the same as we waited, listening to light rock music and each other's breathing.

The nurse came back on the line. "It's positive," she said.

I asked her about ten times if she was sure. The next morning I went back to the lab to ask for a retest. They explained to me how very rare it would be to get a false positive and reassured me that I was indeed pregnant. I wanted to tell them the reason I was so concerned about the accuracy of the test results was because we were also applying for adoption but I didn't mention it. I left the lab walking on a cloud. I was pregnant. Finally pregnant.

That weekend we talked excitedly about all the changes that were about to take place in our lives. For four days I was brimming with excitement. I was finally pregnant.

On the fifth day I began some spotty bleeding. When I called the doctor's office, they said this was not uncommon and that I should stay off my feet for a few days. I got so busy tying up loose ends at my law office that I never actually got around to getting off my feet.

On the sixth day the spotting turned into bleeding. On the seventh day the doctor told me to check into the hospital.

The only time my husband left my side was when I went for an ultrasound. The rest of the time we held hands, cried, and prayed. Words were meaningless. Even the nurse who took care of me felt uncomfortable muttering her sympathy. She handed me a pamphlet on miscarriage and left us alone.

When we left for home, I was no longer pregnant. That week passed in a fog. Neither one of us knew quite what to say, but we did our best to comfort each other. God knew what was best for us. We had to continue to trust in his plan for our lives.

Family and friends were wonderful. There were lots of phone calls and invitations. Someone sent a large flower arrangement. We accepted a few invitations from trusted friends and tried to talk about this little person who had been with us for such a brief time. We loved that little baby, as strange as that may seem, and now it was no more.

I went right back to work on Monday. Physically I felt fine. Emotionally it was rougher. I figured it was best to get back into the swing of things. I blamed myself for the miscarriage. If only I had stayed off my feet for a few days. If only . . .

Life went on. My in-laws arrived for an unexpected visit a week after the miscarriage. They had planned a vacation elsewhere, but severe weather forced them to cancel those plans.

The very next day we got word from a lawyer friend that a certain unborn baby might soon become available for adoption. Were we interested? he asked.

When the shock wore off, we answered with a resounding YES! Our dream of becoming a family was on the verge of coming true. The next day the birth mother delivered a beautiful baby girl.

In Illinois the law provides that consents to adoption cannot be taken until seventy-two hours after delivery. We counted the minutes. My mother-in-law and I tried to get the house ready for a baby.

On the day after the baby's birth, my husband and I sneaked into the hospital to take a peek at her. Her birth mother knew we would be coming, but it felt odd seeing this beautiful baby girl, whom we hoped would be our daughter, and knowing that her birth mother was right across the hall, recovering physically and emotionally behind a closed hospital door. We whispered a quick prayer that she would find some comfort in her grief. Then we turned our attention to the little girl, peering at her through the glass that separated us.

On the third day we went back to the hospital. The birth mother had gone home the day before. The lawyer had arranged for us to have some baby care education. We were all optimistic that the consents would be signed without a hitch later that afternoon. Once they were delivered to the hospital, we could bring the baby home immediately.

We arrived way too early. My husband's parents and my sister and her husband went with us. While my husband and I watched videos and talked to the nurses, our waiting relatives paced and made innumerable trips to the store for last-minute baby items. In between videos, we stood at the nursery window and watched the little girl who would soon be our daughter. One time when we walked away, she flailed one of her little arms and I told my husband that she was waving at us to come get her.

Finally the lawyer arrived with the consents. Everything had gone smoothly. The birth parents were confident and secure in their decision. The attorney handed me a letter and told me to read it later.

We all crowded into a room and watched while the nurse changed and dressed the baby in the outfit we had chosen for her trip home. There was not a dry eye in the place as we watched this precious little girl squirm while being dressed to leave the hospital. Then the nurse wrapped her in blankets and carried her out of the hospital with our entourage following. In the parking lot she handed the baby over to our lawyer. The lawyer handed her to me and for the first time I held my beautiful baby girl.

Tears blurred our vision as we drove the short distance to our home. My poor, distracted husband refused to drive more than five miles an hour and had trouble keeping his eyes on the road.

At home we unwrapped this little bundle to get acquainted. We counted fingers and toes and drank in her eye and hair color. We fought over who would hold her. She was perfect in every way and absolutely beautiful.

Visitors floated through the house during our baby's first evening at home. We couldn't stop crying our tears of joy. We were doubly blessed because my in-laws were there to share the experience and get to know their latest grandchild, all because a storm had disrupted their other plans. God perfectly planned for them to share this moment with us. We couldn't stop hugging each other.

As the evening quieted down, we got out the letter the lawyer had given us at the hospital. It was from our daughter's birth mother, who wanted us to know that she had given the child to us out of love. She hoped that we would tell our daughter that someday. We wish we could tell the birth mother that we often pray for her. Our prayer is that she will experience peace with her decision and be assured of the well-being of her daughter.

We share regularly with Clare the story of her arrival. When she is older she will have access to other information, like the letter from her birth mother. We have a life-story box for Clare. Enclosed in the box is the little cap she wore at the hospital, her first pacifier, her first photo, and all the greetings and good wishes that poured in to welcome her into the world. We add to the box things that tell of milestones in her life. We tell her daily and will continue to tell her that she is a miracle—and proof positive of God's grace and love.

When Clare was ten months old, I discovered that I was three months pregnant, all without the benefit of a basal thermometer or charts. In a very short time we were the parents of two beautiful girls just seventeen months apart in age. Caitlin, our second daughter, was born during an ice storm on a blustery day in March. She came into our lives with a lion's roar but is God's blessing of another little lamb for our family. We have loved every minute of the daily trials of life with two small children. Sometimes the stress has been overwhelming, but we have always kept our focus on the blessing of these little lives.

When Caitlin was slightly over two years old, baby fever struck again. Now thirty-seven years old, I wondered if God was willing to work another miracle for us. We began once again in earnest to contact adoption agencies and gather information.

After doing our homework, we applied for an international adoption from Korea through Bethany Christian Services. Because of our ages and the present status of our family, we were acceptable candidates for international adoption. We relished the idea of becoming a larger, more diverse family. The paperwork and interviews went smoothly. We met some wonderful people and learned some things about each other in the home study process.

We are experts at waiting. Our years of dealing with infertility and adoption have taught us to pray our most fervent prayers and wait patiently for God's reply. We asked him to show us his will for the expansion of our family and were confident in his faithfulness in the large things of life as well as the small.

After the excitement of the application process came the dreaded wait. There were long, dry months and sometimes we thought the process would never end. But even during the dry times, God was faithful in the small things of our lives. Our tossed-off, faintly whispered prayers for small needs were answered swiftly, surely, and faithfully. Even in the tiniest details of our lives, God showed us his grace. And so we continued to wait for this baby, perhaps the last child we would have the privilege to raise.

The year of 1994 was drawing to a close. While watching the changing season and coloring fall pictures with our two little girls, we got the phone call telling us that my husband's sister had been murdered by her estranged husband. "Not in our family!" we protested. "Why would God do this to us?" we cried, questioning his wisdom and his ways.

We will never understand some of the things that happen to us, but through the large things and the small, our God is faithful. The family gathered to plan a beautiful memorial for Phyllis. We shared love, hope, and prayers in our unexpected week together and always felt the strong, sure hand of God holding us together and holding us up to give us the strength to face this tragedy.

We arrived back at my in-laws' house in Michigan after the funeral to find a message on the answering machine. "This is Bethany Christian calling. Can you call us back right away?"

With extension phones in hand, we heard our social worker say that they had a baby girl for us. In fact, she had gotten the referral from Korea on the morning that Phyllis was killed but hadn't been able to call that day because she needed some more information before the referral was official.

Our tears of sorrow were once again mixed with tears of joy as she described the tiny baby girl who had been born a few months earlier and who would soon be joining our family. We were able to give my husband's grieving parents new hope: the anticipation of a new life joining the family for all of us to treasure. Through her tears over the loss of her own daughter, my mother-in-law began making plans to sew matching dresses for our daughters to wear to a baby dedication at my in-laws' church. The news of this new life had brought us all back to a point of hope and expectancy.

We returned home to Illinois and went to the adoption agency's office, where we received photos of a beautiful little girl who weighed only five and one-half pounds at birth. We longed to hold her and to make her smile. "Will she cry in Korean?" the two big sisters asked, who were then three and one-half and five years old.

A few months of waiting loomed ahead of us. We accepted our baby's referral at the end of October 1994. She arrived in our arms on February 9, 1995, at five months of age.

We gathered at the airport on that cold morning with three other couples, each absorbed in their private anticipation. No one felt much like chatting.

The adoption agency had instructed us to bring a blanket to the airport. Greeters would board the airplane, retrieve the babies from their escorts, wrap them in their family's blanket, and carry them through customs to their waiting parents. When we spotted our blanket, we would know which baby was ours and which greeter to mob with our welcoming shrieks.

The "big" girls paced with us while we waited for our baby. When the greeter walked into the waiting area, we swarmed around her in delirious excitement. Wrapped in our blanket was our beautiful, very healthy baby daughter. She had obviously been well cared for by her foster mother, as she was nearly twice the size we had anticipated. The tiny baby clothing we had arranged would be replaced with a larger size. We stuffed her into her pram suit and began the long drive home. We will be forever grateful for the love and care of her foster mother in Korea.

Two of our children were complete surprises and the last was planned and anticipated. But in all things, large and small, God has been faithful to us. We have named this latest child Grace. We remain always faithful to God and each of our children is an unexpected, undeserved blessing from him. We will raise them to know and love the Lord, so that they too may daily experience his unmerited favor in their lives.

What about your family? Are you struggling with fertility issues? Do you have the "just one more baby" blues? Is there room in your heart to love a little human being who needs nurture and guidance?

If you answered yes to any of these questions, then maybe adoption is for you. You need solid, reliable, current information to make the many decisions ahead of you. With your fervent prayer and a little practical guidance, God will show you the way to build your family.

 **TWO**

Getting Started

As a Christian, I know that God has a perfect plan for our lives and that he perfectly arranges events and circumstances for us. The psalmist said, "My frame was not hidden from you when I was made in the secret place. When I was woven together in the depths of the earth, your eyes saw my unformed body. All the days ordained for me were written in your book before one of them came to be" (Ps. 139:15–16). God puts imperfect parents in touch with children who need love and a home, and it works beautifully.

As I write this book, we are contemplating the adoption of a fourth child. It is not a logical, reasonable thing to consider, given our ages, our living situation, and our finances. Yet the desire to love one more child is burning in my heart! My prayer is that God will either show the way or remove the desire from my heart. It is in his hands and we await his guidance. That is the only way to approach adoption. At some point, it is completely out of your control and you must accept in faith God's will for your life.

The First Steps

The process of adopting can be intimidating. I have talked to many couples who have put off even beginning an inquiry because of the complexity of the information and options available. "Adoption can be compared to going through a maze," say Connie Crain and Janice Duffy.[1] Parents may become misdirected and confused trying to navigate their way. We often felt like hamsters running a maze going through our process but soon realized that the sooner we got in step and did the necessary work, the sooner we would reach the reward at the end of the maze.

Our first adoption was a marvelous, blessed, miraculous godsend. I doubt that a similar experience will ever be repeated for us, although God has sent us many miracles since. When we decided to expand our family beyond two children, we knew that we would have to try a more common route. We knew a little about Korean adoption and thought it might be a good idea. We had a lot to learn but we plunged in eagerly.

Before settling on a specific agency for our second adoption, we went to several informational sessions offered by adoption agencies. These free orientations, usually held at a convenient evening time, are an excellent way to gather information and educate yourself about the adoption process. In fact, some agencies require attendance at a meeting before you can even receive an information and application packet. Look at this as merely the first in a series of hoops to jump through to get to the goal of your child. It is also your initial chance to meet other couples in the same circumstance. These couples will share the waiting game with you. You can learn from their research and experience, as well as share thoughts of your own.

Informational meetings are attended by all kinds of people—all with their own hopes and dreams for a family. Some will come away from the meeting overwhelmed and discouraged. The social workers say they will "self-select out." Others will become tenacious. Our motto became, "Show us the hoops to jump through *now* so that we can get to jumping."

A great way to start your research on adoption is to send for a free publication distributed by Adoptive Families of America (AFA) called *Guide to Adoption*. It is regularly updated and lists agencies and parent support groups by state. The contact information is current and accurate. It also provides a basic introduction to the adoption process. AFA also publishes a bimonthly magazine called *Adoptive Families* (see appendix A for the address and phone number).

You can also use the internet to help you in your adoption journey. One resource is AdoptioNetwork. On it you can locate agencies, do basic research, and even run an ad to try to locate a birth mother. This is an exciting trend for the adoption community, but please exercise caution in the use of the internet. While it can be a blessing to have this kind of exposure in your quest, it can also provide a fertile field for scam operators. As with every other avenue you travel, verify information and ask for references.

Authors Wirth and Worden suggest setting a time frame for research, such as one to three months.[2] During this time, gather as much information as possible and try to meet and talk with other adoptive families (perhaps through an adoption support group). After assembling all available information, evaluate what you have learned. Sort out your impressions of agencies and workers you have met. Have you found someone with whom you have a good fit? Do you trust his or her competency, honesty, and compassion? At this point you may even conclude that adoption is not an option and you can close this chapter in your life. Or you may gain a real sense of direction and be armed with the information and enthusiasm to proceed.

There is no doubt that the process of adoption requires large doses of patience, prayer, perseverance, and humor.

Keep your eyes on that child who may someday join your family, and move ahead.

The Statistics

The numbers vary at any given time as to couples seeking a child and as to infertile couples in this country. An estimate from the early 1990s was that a million couples were seeking to adopt each year, and of that number only one in thirty would get a baby.[3] In the mid-1990s, for every baby available for adoption there were forty couples seeking to adopt.[4] Statistics can be manipulated. Whether the odds are thirty to one or forty to one, there *are* children to adopt.

In 1988 Marlys Harris concluded that "there is a larger pool of potentially adoptable babies and children than at any time in the nation's history. The number of illegitimate births has more than doubled to nearly 880,000 since the Supreme Court upheld women's right to abortion in 1973."[5] She says that the news of a shortage of children causes many couples to lose hope and to enter into a gray market of adoption that is controlled by lawyers and baby brokers. Clearly, there are children available. Some are older, some are of minority races, and some have special needs. They all need homes, along with the many "perfect and normal" infants who become available for adoption each year.

Some couples don't bother to research because of several factors: (1) they have heard the accounts of long waits and have become discouraged; (2) they don't know where to start their quest; (3) they feel that the costs involved are prohibitive, even though they may be misinformed; (4) they don't consider researching adoption while they are continuing to try to conceive; or (5) they are dissuaded by the legal horror stories they have heard in the media concerning adoption. When research is begun in earnest, many of these fears can be resolved.

Experts admit that the number of couples in the adoption marketplace is uncertain. In 1988 William Pierce, president of the National Committee for Adoption, claimed that there were forty infertile couples for every adoptable child. This statement is based on his estimate that there were two million infertile couples and there were fifty thousand adoptions in 1982, making the ratio forty to one. When questioned about these numbers, Pierce admitted that they were "soft numbers" but were being reported by the media as hard facts.[6] The article's author referred to the numbers as "squishy" and went on to point out that about half of all infertile couples eventually conceive, so only about five hundred thousand of those infertile couples were truly potential adoptive parents. This shift in the numbers increases the odds considerably and illustrates how little faith should be placed on odds.

Another article painted an even bleaker picture. In 1987 author Lewis Lord postulated that "10 million Americans—1 couple in 6 of childbearing age—are defined as infertile. That is, they have tried for a year or more to achieve successful pregnancy and haven't."[7] If all of those infertile couples sought adoption, the odds would be almost astronomical against anyone ever adopting. Of course any figures related to infertility are "squishy," to use another's description. This is a highly private, personal matter, and not all infertile couples seek to adopt.

Yet in 1992, the last year for which complete statistics are available, there were 127,441 adoptions, according to the National Adoption Information Clearinghouse. Those adoptions were varied. For example, 42 percent were stepparent or relative adoptions, 15.5 percent were through public agencies, 5 percent were international adoptions, and the balance of 37.5 percent were through a private agency or an independent adoption.

The numbers speak for themselves. It is simply not true that there aren't any children available. Someone is adopting these children. Why not you?

THREE

Adoption Law

It may seem odd to begin a discussion about how to adopt with an overview of adoption law, but being educated is being forewarned. As an attorney, I believe we must have a consumer mind-set about adoption. Check all your options. Verify any information you receive, even from books written by lawyers! The more educated you are about the process and the possibilities, the greater the likelihood of a positive outcome.

This brief overview should help you to evaluate the advisability of getting into an adoptive situation when there is the possibility that it will not have a happy ending and to track the progress of your adoption case until its completion. Although many lawyers resent the well-informed consumer, remember that you are indeed a consumer of legal services and you are usually paying for them handsomely as well. If something seems unusual or if you are not comfortable with the way something is being handled, ask questions and stay informed. This is the only way to celebrate a complete, uncompromised, joyous adoption.

The media's excessive coverage of certain adoption disasters should not discourage consideration of adoption. It is important for adoptive parents to have familiarity with adoption law. At the very least, parents should know how a consent is taken and under what circumstances that consent may be withdrawn. Increasing attention needs to be paid to birth fathers and the termination of their parental rights. This chapter includes brief discussions of these issues.

We often have a blind trust in those professionals whose services we use. If you have a disease, it is wise to read all that you can about the disease so that you can converse knowledgeably about it with doctors who specialize in treating the disease. Adoption can be just as mysterious as medical treatments. The more you know, the better position you will be in to evaluate potential opportunities that come your way.

While it is important for you to be familiar with the law, it is imperative that adoptive parents have competent legal counsel. Your brother-in-law who just finished law school and did an adequate job on your real-estate closing may not be in the best position to advise you on your adoption. Similarly, your experienced, trusted real-estate attorney may not be familiar with adoption law. The earlier that expert counsel is consulted, the fewer legal problems will be encountered.

I am often asked, "At what point should I consult an adoption attorney?" The answer is, "Now." Your attorney can help you evaluate your possibilities and guide you every step of the way.

Many of the cases that have caught media attention have been ones in which the consents were improperly or untimely taken or adoptive parents misunderstood the extent of their rights in the early phases of an adoption. Many of these errors were avoidable. A consent is the legal document by which the birth parents relinquish all of their rights to the child. In many states, there is a waiting period after the birth before the consent may be executed. There may also be a period of time during which the consents can be contested because they were obtained under fraud or duress. There is more on these matters later in the chapter.

No one is more motivated than you to protect your adoption and to make certain everything is done ethically and legally. It is up to you to be familiar with the legal process of adoption and to protect yourselves as well as your child.

Lawyers and Their Fees

Most lawyers are ethically obligated to have you sign an up-front fee agreement that describes the services they will provide and how fees will be structured. In a typical arrangement, a lawyer will charge an initial retainer fee, then you will agree to pay a certain hourly rate for time spent after that retainer fee has been exhausted. With a smooth adoption, your lawyer should be able to tell you a maximum fee for his or her services.

Keep in mind, however, that this probably will not include fees for contested hearings. If the birth father balks or if the birth mother attempts to withdraw her consent (which is extremely unlikely), your fees could skyrocket.

You need to have these possibilities spelled out for you as early as possible to avoid a billing shock later in the process. Ask at the onset what your lawyer's dollar figure would be for his or her representation in a worst-case scenario.

In a private adoption, the expenses of the birth mother are always an issue. Most states allow payment of medical expenses by adoptive parents, typically after the consents are signed. As with anything else, check with your lawyer, because if you do not adhere to the law at any point in your proceedings, you jeopardize your adoption. With regard to medical expenses, beware of signing any document by which you guarantee the payment of the birth mother's medical and legal expenses. No matter how committed she may seem, no matter how smoothly the process may be going, if she decides to keep her child and you have committed yourself to guaranteeing these expenses, you will be legally responsible for them. Your odds of then collecting those expenses from the birth mother are slim.

Investigate whether the birth mother you are working with has private insurance or is eligible for Medicaid. If she is willing to submit these claims (which is perfectly legal even if the child is placed for adoption), you can realize a substantial savings in your adoption budget.

Some states allow the payment of reasonable living expenses to the birth mother. Usually these arrangements are under very controlled circumstances requiring court approval. Make sure your lawyer has thoroughly researched your state's law on this issue and that it is being followed scrupulously. You may be required to seek court authority prior to any such payment or file affidavits with regard to each payment or both. Following a sloppy procedure in this arena could be both costly and illegal. In any event, you should never make any payment to the birth mother directly. Payments should be handled by your attorney as your intermediary.

Consents or Surrenders

Before a child becomes available to adopt, either through an agency or a private adoption, legal consents must be signed by the birth parents. State laws vary, but most consents are signed within three or four days after the birth of the child. Formal consents mean that the baby is given over to your care or to the care of a foster parent, pending a final completion of the adoption. They terminate the legal rights of the birth parents. If you are adopting through an agency, the agency will take care of the consents. If you are adopting independently, make sure utmost care is taken in the execution of the consents by your adoption professionals.

The consents must be signed voluntarily, without fraud, duress, or the influence of drugs or alcohol. Your state may require that the consents be taken in front of a notary public, judge, or both. These documents must be executed with the greatest care, as they form the basis for your adoption court case. With signed consents, the formal legal work for your adoption can begin.

In some states birth parents have a certain period of time in which to rescind their consent. In other states, the consents are irrevocable if signed properly. Make sure you know which law exists in your state.

If the child has been abandoned or abused, the birth mother is in jail, or the birth father is not paying support, there may not be voluntarily signed consents, and a court hearing could be held for the *involuntary* legal termination of parental rights. If birth parents or their families show any interest in or concern for the child at all, there could be a drawn out legal battle. Make sure you are prepared financially and emotionally to fight.

The Rights of Birth Fathers

The law as to the rights of birth fathers varies from state to state and depends on the nature of the relationship between the birth father and mother. In *Stanley v. Illinois* (405 US. 645, 92 S. Ct. 1208, 31 L.Ed. 2d 551, 1972) the United States Supreme Court ruled that the Constitution requires that a birth father be given notice that he may be the father of a child who is to be adopted and be given an opportunity to be heard. The type of notice or consent required from the birth father depends on his relationship to the mother.

For example, if the birth father was married to the birth mother within a designated period of time before the birth, many states require his written consent. Even if they were not married, he may have those same rights if he lived with the birth mother after he became aware of the pregnancy.

If the birth father was never married to or never lived with the birth mother, many states will not require his written consent but rather will require that he be given formal notice that an adoption is pending. After notification, he may object to the adoption by filing a petition to establish his parentage within a specified period, usually thirty days. If he does not take any action during this period, his parental rights can be terminated automatically and the adoption case can go forward without further notice to him. If a father does choose to object to the adoption, then the court will hold a hearing to determine what is in the child's best interest.

In most cases birth fathers do not oppose adoptions, but great care must be exercised in this area so as not to compromise the finality of the adoption. This may have been the problem in several failed adoption cases. The parties involved had not been diligent about notification to birth fathers or the birth mother may have lied about the status of the father. These recent legal horror stories will be discussed in a later chapter. For now suffice it to say that such tragedies only happen in an *extremely* small number of cases.

Why is such care and attention paid to the rights of birth fathers? There are several reasons. The smoothest adoptions are ones in which both birth parents consent freely. If the birth father is absent or unknown, there may be future challenges to the adoption after its completion.

In addition, it is wise to involve a birth father early on because a child deserves to be raised with a full history. Many times adoptive parents are only given a medical and social history for the birth mother, if they are given any background information at all. This ignores the fact that the child has an entire genetic and cultural heritage from the birth father as well. This can be crucial information when there are inherited diseases or other conditions that the adoptive parents need to monitor.

Here are some red flags to watch for in the area of birth fathers: (1) the mother cannot identify the father; (2) the mother has had multiple partners and does not know which one is the father; (3) the mother refuses to identify the birth father. Each of these situations must be handled carefully and according to your state's law.

What if the identity or whereabouts of the birth father are unknown? If the birth father is known but he cannot be located, in most states a formal notice must be published in the legal section of a newspaper informing persons of the pending adoption and of their legal right to appear in court to oppose the adoption. If the court is satisfied that the adoptive parents have exercised due diligence or reasonable efforts to locate the birth father, the case may continue.

If the identity of the birth father is truly unknown, most courts will terminate the rights of an unknown father and allow the case to proceed.

Some states have a registry that puts the burden of claims to paternity on the father. He must register with the state if he believes he is the father of a child potentially placed for adoption. If he fails to register, he loses the right to contest adoption proceedings.

Every state has a statutory requirement compelling fathers to support their children. If a child born out of wedlock is not placed for adoption, the birth mother has the right to sue the father for paternity and child support, and his obligation to support continues until the child marries or reaches the age of eighteen.

If a birth mother keeps the child and files for some form of welfare, the local authorities are required, under federal law, to sue the birth father for paternity and child support, *whether the mother wants to sue him or not.* These support cases are often vigorously pursued by the government, and a birth father may see his wages garnished or attached.

It is no surprise that birth fathers are often relieved to see a child placed for adoption. If at all possible, birth fathers should be actively involved in the adoption process and receive counseling with the birth mother to avoid many of the scenarios above.

If a birth father is concerned that the child is not his biological child, there is a blood test, called an HLA (Human Leucocyte Antigen) test, that can establish paternity with about 99.8 percent accuracy. These results are legally recognized as admissible in court and may be helpful in persuading an uncooperative father who doubted his paternity to voluntarily waive his paternal rights.

The Petition to Adopt

After you have obtained consents and been approved through the home study process—if a home study is required—you are ready to file a petition to adopt, which is your legal request to the court asking that your adoption be completed or finalized. There will be a final hearing, usually in a judge's chambers or a closed courtroom. Final hearings tend to be very informal and are times for joyous celebration. Make it a family affair! Have guests accompany you and take pictures of the judge and lawyers to save for your child's life-story book or memory box. This is a day to remember. You will tell this story to your child many, many times.

At some point after your final hearing you will obtain a Judgment of Adoption. This does not mean the legal work is done. You will still need to obtain a birth certificate from your local Department of Vital Records, a social security number, and, in the case of international adoption, citizenship papers.

On application, your state will issue an amended birth certificate that gives the new name of the child and lists you as parents. It may give the child's birthplace, but it will not have any information about the birth parents nor give any indication that the child is adopted. When you reach this point and are ordering the certified copy of the birth certificate, order several extra copies. You will need them for all sorts of events in your child's life, such as school entry, getting a driver's license, or getting married.

Avoiding Trouble

Some cases of birth mother scams have recently been highlighted by the media. These involve women who contact several adoptive parents with the promise of surrendering their baby. They often collect a lot of money and then disappear. In some cases, the woman was not even pregnant. Author Nancy Reynolds offers five precautions:

a. If you are using a facilitator, check their references carefully.
b. Verify the pregnancy. Ask for a letter from the birth mother's doctor confirming the pregnancy, due date, and health of the mother and child to the extent known.
c. Ask the birth mother for personal and/or employment references and verify them.
d. Let the birth parents know that you are aware of state adoption laws and that you intend to comply with them.
e. If you are allowed to pay certain expenses such as medical bills, make arrangements for you to be given copies of the bills so you can verify each before paying for it.[1]

I would add to these precautions that in many states you need court authority to pay any expenses and you must strictly comply with these requirements.

Some of these points are common sense, but adoptive parents may become swept away in the emotion of the situation and may not exercise the best judgment. Be careful. If a birth mother appears to lack any connection to her own family or if she seems to be working in tandem with her boyfriend, these are warning signs, especially if she expresses a desire to marry the boyfriend. "If she doesn't show up for appointments, if she doesn't sign papers right away, if she acts as if she is doing you a favor, it means she doesn't value adoption," notes Michael Sullivan.[2] Any of these signs spell trouble for your adoption, whether by fraud or by an indecisive mother. For the peace of mind of all the parties involved, proceed with extreme caution if any of these signs materialize in your situation.

Attorney Randall Hicks lists several factors to check.

1. Birth mother's due date. If it is far in the future, she may be premature in making her adoptive plan.
2. Personal motivations. If the birth mother is placing the child at the request of an angry parent or to placate a boyfriend, she will have to come to terms with these competing pressures. This could spell disaster for you.
3. Financial assistance. If the birth mother makes unreasonable requests for funds, her motivation may be to enhance her lifestyle, not make a plan for her child.
4. Counseling. If an adoption professional discourages counseling for the birth mother, proceed with caution.
5. Does she know her options? If a birth mother has not explored options to placing her child for adoption, she may explore them later after the placement of her child. This could cause her to have second thoughts. Better she know her options up front.
6. Her age. The younger the birth mother, the less prepared she will be for the emotional upheaval of birth.
7. Feelings of the birth father. Usually they are in favor of adoption, but if he has shown a high interest in the child and opposes the adoption, this is a major red flag.[3]

Several years ago I counseled a couple who made a private arrangement with a birth mother without the aid of an agency or intermediary to work with both sides. Despite my cautions to the couple, they took the baby home before legal consents were signed. The birth mother signed the baby out of the hospital, then handed her over to the adoptive parents. The happy couple went home to begin their new life with their new baby.

The very young birth mother returned home to her parents and then proceeded to delay her appointments to sign consents and ultimately changed her mind after the child had been in the adoptive parents' home for ten days. The nursery was decorated, furnishings were bought, and an entire wardrobe purchased. The room remained empty for another three years until I was able to arrange another private adoption for the couple. They now are the happy, secure parents of a six-year-old boy who was placed with them at three days old. In the second instance, they were patient and exercised legal caution. The results were more satisfying for all the parties involved, as the procedure was handled with strict compliance with adoption law.

 # FOUR

Why Adopt?

I need only look at the faces of my daughters to know why we adopted. When I see them holding and playing with their new baby sister, her sweet face gazing adoringly at them, I know that a gracious God had his hand in bringing our family together.

When we began to think about raising a family, I believed I would feel a great loss if I were denied this life experience. My husband and I could have gone through our time on earth focused on each other, our careers, and our pursuits, but there was a void in that scenario. The absence of children made the future look less exciting. When I imagined us as a family, I imagined the whole experience: the crying and the fighting, the earaches and the fevers. I knew intuitively that beyond the struggles and through the struggles there was joy, as evidenced by the sounds of giggling and squeals of delight in a happy home.

We wanted to share our lives with little creations of God and help them grow to live for, love, and serve him. This was our motivation to adopt. Adoption is not about what gifts a child will bring to your life. Rather it is about the joy of giving love and compassion to another human being. It is an act of grace that a tragedy for a birth mother can become a gift of God for an adoptive family. It will cause you to grow in maturity, responsibility, spirituality, and caring for others.

The decision to adopt was easy for us, even though it required much soul searching and honest reflection. For many people, there are many more reasons *not* to adopt. These must be honestly examined, for the sake of the married couple as well as for that of a child potentially joining your family. The wrong reasons to adopt will be discussed first, and then a decision tree will be presented to help determine your readiness to adopt.

Wrong Reasons to Adopt

Wrong reason #1: We will be doing the poor child a favor. On more than one occasion someone has approached me and said, "I think it's wonderful what you're doing."

"What am I doing?" I reply.

"You know. Taking in these poor children and giving them a good Christian home. They are very lucky."

"You've got it all wrong," I respond. "We are the lucky ones." We have been blessed by God with the privilege of raising children. They are his gifts to us.

To think of adoption as a favor to a child focuses on you and the gratitude you may expect from that child. That is a heavy burden to place on a child. A child needs to be loved for who he or she is—a wonderful creation of God—and not for any misguided motivation on the part of parents. Authors Wirth and Worden strongly advise, "If you adopt a child to rescue him or her, you'll wear your son or daughter like a martyr's crown. . . . The only reason to adopt is that you want to become a parent."[1]

Wrong reason #2: Our other child will have a playmate. This could be a valid reason to adopt, depending on your entire motivation. A lady I once met was marveling at how well my first two girls, who are seventeen months apart, play together. This lady had a two-year-old girl and was weary of being her daughter's best playmate. She said to me, "Do you think I could adopt a two-year-old so my little Susie would have someone to play with?"

I tried to explain to her that it was not like renting a video game—when you were done playing with it, you could return it to the store and life would go on. If you are looking for a toy for your other children to play with, or for an accessory for yourself to play with and dress up, you are missing the point. Just hire a neighbor's kid. It's a lot less trouble.

On the other hand, perhaps you have three girls and want to adopt a boy to experience what a boy would bring to your family. Or maybe your dream has always been to have a family of a certain size and there is room in your hearts and home to accommodate this dream. These are perfectly valid reasons to pursue adoption.

Wrong reason #3: We've been through the mill of fertility testing and we deserve a baby. Many couples have gone to enormous lengths to try to conceive, exhausting all biological and hormonal solutions. The disappointment and despair you experience after these options have failed can be so overwhelming as to impair your judgment.

What if the experience of adoption only leads to more disappointment before you are emotionally prepared to cope? On the other hand, could you love and accept an adopted child if you were still harboring bitterness over the disappointment of infertility?

When we began our journey to becoming a family, it really didn't matter to us how our children came to us. However God would see fit to fashion us together, we would accept joyfully, and he has blessed us by giving us three healthy infants so far.

The experience of infertility leaves a couple in an emotionally jangled and mentally drained state. You should consider adoption only after you have dealt with your feelings and grieved over the impact infertility has had on your lives. When you are ready to choose adoption, don't let it be your second choice for building a family. Instead, make sure you are prepared emotionally and spiritually for it to be your best choice.

Wrong reason #4: Raising a baby will help our marriage. Those moments of blissfully rocking a quiet child to sleep are fleeting, few, and far between. Many of the remaining moments are tiring and stressful. They can strain closeness and communication in even the best marriage. If you don't believe this, offer to watch a friend's infant for a weekend. Measure your fatigue level at the end of that time. This will give you a good glimpse of the added stress of having a baby around the house.

Of course, a new family member can and should lead to increased closeness, but the relationship should be on firm footing *before* undertaking such an endeavor. The pressure of adding a baby to an already shaky marriage will only aggravate existing problems, not solve them. Seek some solutions first before considering adoption, for the sake of your marriage as well as for the sake of your child. Children deserve a stable, loving home environment.

Wrong reason #5: Having a baby to raise will make me feel loved and complete. As a Christian, I believe that a personal, loving relationship with Jesus Christ is the only thing that makes me complete and loved. There was a time in my not-too-distant past when I believed that a career, a good husband, and a house full of children would make me feel happy and fulfilled. God has graciously granted me all of these things and they have brought me great joy, but only Jesus has made me whole and redeemed my soul.

While I struggled with infertility, I had an aching in my heart for children. I would have carried great sadness in my life if I were not allowed to raise children, but my basic wholeness and completeness came from my Savior. Life would still have been okay without children. If that had been

God's will for my life, it would have been my task to cheerfully accept that and move on. Perhaps there was other work he had for me to do, like being a foster parent or becoming more deeply involved in children's ministry.

If you want children in your life, there are always ways to get involved. Maybe there is a child in your neighborhood who needs a friend. Maybe you can get involved in work at your church with children or youth. So many children are longing for the interest and attention of an adult. There is no shortage of opportunities for you to get involved with children.

The Bible tells us, "This is the confidence we have in approaching God: that if we ask anything according to his will, he hears us" (1 John 5:14). If you think adoption might be for you, ask God first to bless your inclination and give you direction. Seek first to do his will. The psalmist tells us, "Teach me to do your will, for you are my God" (Ps. 143:10). When we are in his will, he can do an amazing work in our lives and in granting the desires of our heart. If adoption is not in his will, that is a reality that must be faced.

The best life to welcome a child into is a rich, full life grounded in the love of Jesus. If you are not so grounded, open your heart to Christ first. Let him make clear his will for your life.

Wrong reason #6: My spouse really wants a child. It is not a good reason to adopt solely to make someone else happy. If your spouse has always wanted children but you don't, *don't adopt.* If your parents are anxious for grandchildren and you want only to make them happy, *don't adopt.* If your friends are pressuring you to join the ranks of over-worked parents, think long and hard first! It is not a good reason to adopt solely to prove something to others or to make someone else happy. The joy your spouse has at the addition of a new life to your family should be shared by you.

Wrong reason #7: Adopting a child will help us to conceive our "own" child. Fertility issues must be sorted out separately from the desire to adopt if adoption is to be entered into freely and clearly.

The anecdotes of increased fertility after adoption are legion. Indeed, it happened in my own family. Yet, Strom and Donnelly say,

> Statistical studies have found that of those families who have been told by their doctors that they are infertile and cannot have a child, eight percent will prove the doctors wrong and give birth to a child anyway. The same, and other, studies have found that among adopting families about eight percent will give birth to a child. Obviously, we are talking about the same eight percent of proving the doctors wrong. Adoption has nothing to do with fertility.[2]

Another social worker put it this way: "Adoption is not a solution to infertility. . . . It is a solution to the question of parenting."[3]

Even though our family fit into the 8 percent who conceived almost immediately after adoption, it was a bittersweet adjustment. As illogical as it sounds, I felt I had somehow let down my first adopted child by having a newborn biological infant to care for. My first daughter had been the one to help heal my broken heart from infertility and dashed dreams, and how dare I immediately have a biological child when I wasn't done raising that beautiful first child! I felt I had done something terribly wrong to her. Those feelings passed and we now are grateful to have each child with her own unique gifts and attributes, but there were some irrational emotions to contend with at the beginning. As always, God provided the wisdom, patience, and discernment to deal with the situation.

I did not initially adopt to increase the odds of conceiving. That should not be your motivation, either. If that is what God has planned for you, however, you can embrace it joyously and thank him for many blessings—after you recover from the shock!

Sorting out Fantasy and Reality

Adopters are risk-takers. The process of adoption does not guarantee a child, much less a perfect child or a perfect family life. Life holds no such guarantees, either for birth parents or adoptive parents. Yet birth parents seem more willing to accept a less than ideal child. "He gets that annoying habit from Uncle Charlie," they might console themselves. It is easier to accept a difficult child who shares your biological heritage, it seems. "That's just the way we are in this family," I have heard parents comment.

That is why it is so crucial to examine your motivation at the outset. The process of adoption as well as the process of parenting an adopted child are not for everyone. It is best to sort out the fantasy from the reality of both.

Your adopted child may not be perfect. He will have flaws and habits that drive you to distraction, and so do biological children. You have to be ready to accept everything about that child before you can fully accept him into your heart. Your love for him cannot in any way be inferior to your love for a biological child. He cannot be allowed to feel he is in any way second best.

Each child is unique and a special gift from God. One of my children is biological and the others are adopted. The biological one is no more like me than the others. I wouldn't expect her to be. They all have their individual personalities. Seeing those personalities unfold is one of the joys of parenting. We have the privilege of having a bird's-eye view of their blossoming.

It would be accurate to say I loved the "idea" of each of my children before I loved them. I fantasized about how each of them would look and how each of them would act. They all surprised me and they all at times make it difficult to love them. But the love comes from the commitment that is part of the process of caring for a child, getting to know a child, and sharing your life with a child. Our feelings about our children may change from minute to minute, along with their mercurial blossoming personalities, but our unconditional love for them cannot waver.

Sherry Bunin notes, "In general our society appears to view adopted children and their families with suspicion." Many people think adoption creates a risky family situation—"as if adoption were a game of chance, a wheel of fortune, unlike any other serious decision in life."[4] The fact of the matter is that most adopted kids turn out just fine. An adoptive family is no more pathological than a biological one. They're each equally risky, scary, challenging, and subject to the influence of genetic factors that drive behavior. Family life has its ups and downs, no matter how the family was formed, but it is infinitely worthwhile.

In those rare families for whom adoption has been a disappointment, the disappointment can be traced to failed expectations. One writer says, "When adoptive families come to grief, it is often from a disparity in expectations; either the parents expected something the child cannot deliver, or the child delivers something the parents did not expect."[5] It is the fantasy of the perfect child that must be reckoned with, along with the fantasy of being perfect parents. Neither exists.

An Adoption Decision Tree

Is adoption for you? I read an interesting statistic that said, "It's usually about a year from the time a couple begins discussing adoption to making that first phone call. The idea emerges as a seed thought and appears to grow and gather energy."[6] You have nothing to lose by gathering information and praying for God's will for your life. What follows is a matrix for you and your spouse to assess where you fall in the adoption decision-making process.

| My spouse and I agree that adoption is how we will build our family. | If no $\Longrightarrow$ | Continue to talk, think, pray, and study. |

If yes, go on ⇓

| Our marriage is stable and secure. | If no $\Longrightarrow$ | Go for marriage counseling first. A child deserves a stable home. |

If yes, go on ⇓

| My spouse and I are emotionally healthy and have basically resolved our fertility issues. | If no $\Longrightarrow$ | Get some professional counseling. You need to be emotionally healthy to withstand the adoption process and to be an effective parent. |

If yes, go on ⇓

| We have decided on which type of adoption to pursue: infant, older, special needs, domestic, or international. | If no $\Longrightarrow$ | Continue to read, research, send for information from agencies and groups, and attend informational meetings. |

If yes, go on ⇓

| We have the financial ability to pay for an adoption. | If no $\Longrightarrow$ | Check into liquidation of assets, borrowing from friends, relatives, lenders, or obtaining a home equity loan. If adopting a special needs child, check with your state welfare authorities and your agency for funding assistance. |

If yes, go on ⇓

Begin the application process!

Adoption Decision Tree
Figure 1

Grace

As Christians, we view adoption as an act of grace. A childless couple is given an opportunity to love and nurture a human being who has been born to another. This exchange and sharing of one need for another, of one sacrifice for another's opportunity, can only be explained and accepted as a function of God's grace.

Parents who adopt volunteer to accept that grace. Author Jayne Schooler notes:

> Adoption is not only voluntary; it is also redemptive. "Redeem" means to release, to make up for, to restore. An adoptive family's guiding light is the vision to restore to an abused or neglected child the dignity of life that was ripped from him. It is a dignity that child was born to enjoy.[7]

Just as a child's future can be redeemed by adoption, so too can the broken hearts of childless couples be redeemed.

This is a particularly profound principle as it relates to the adoption of special needs children. Parents who adopt these children see the inherent value of their lives—they see beyond the problems and see a child who is worthy of love and dignity simply because he is a creation of God.

Just as by God's grace we are accepted into his family with unconditional love, when we adopt we do the same for a child. God is the perfect model for our parenting, and we can ask him to help allay any fears we have about loving an adopted child.

Douglas R. Donnelly, an attorney and adoptive parent himself, says it this way:

> To take two separate tragedies—an unplanned pregnancy and a couple grieving over an infertility problem—and to combine them in such a way as to solve both problems simultaneously, is exciting beyond words. Through grace, the birth mother makes a painful but heroic decision and is granted

the strength to see the decision through. Also through grace, the adopting parents accept a child into their home and bestow on that child their name, their material possessions and the fullest measure of their love and affection. A special bond exists between birth mothers and adopting parents. They have together, through teamwork of a most magnificent kind, created a human being with a soul and personality, in a way which neither could have accomplished without the other. There is no greater human example of grace.[8]

The Joy of Children

In your decision-making process don't forget the exceptional joy that children can bring. Children add a life dimension that may be experienced no other way. It matters not if those children are biological, adopted, foster, or in some other way mentored by you.

There is a special way that a child can love a significant adult that is unlike any other love you may experience. The reciprocal is also true. Bruce Rappaport says:

> Most parents find that the most powerful part of parenting is not how deeply their children love them, but how extraordinary it feels to love their child. Outside of parenting, few people experience the absolute, unconditional, and overwhelming quality of the love they feel for a son or daughter. There is purity and joy in the love of a child that is fundamentally different from other forms of love.[9]

Loving a child, however that child comes into your life, is clearly more about giving than about getting. It is about the giving of unconditional love.

One researcher studied 104 sets of first-time parents—52 biological and 52 adoptive. In interviews before and after the arrival of the babies, the adoptive parents reported "more satisfying experiences" than did natural parents. She concludes that after battling the frustration of infertility, such couples are more appreciative of the rewards—and changes—a child can bring to their lives. Besides, "people who adopt are usually older and more mature and have been married longer than natural parents, which makes them better able to handle the stresses of parenthood."[10]

Are You Ready?

There is no way to truly anticipate the changes that a child will bring to a home. The amount of time and work involved always comes as a surprise.

Author Elaine Walker looks at some of the freedoms you give up when you become a parent. Among them are the freedom to come and go as you please; the freedom to sleep, make love, read, watch TV, and relax without interruptions; the freedom of providing just for yourself; and the freedom to pursue your career to the fullest.[11]

There is an aspect of readiness on the part of the parents that must exist before you should consider adoption. Some of that readiness involves feeling comfortable with having exhausted fertility treatment or deciding that it is simply more important to become a parent than to become pregnant. Some of that readiness involves feeling like it is time to throw away the thermometers and the fertility charts and the intimacy-on-a-schedule lifestyle you may have led for years. It is the feeling that enough is enough!

It is a readiness for closure of that chapter of your life that has involved desperately seeking biological pregnancy and fully embracing alternative means of achieving parenthood. For us, the readiness was an unbridled excitement at the prospect of raising a baby (my husband says it was unbridled excitement and sheer terror)!

Social workers who have dealt extensively with adoption can distinguish between "good adopters" and those who are not quite ready. A "good adopter" is enthusiastic about the process; has a stable life and lifestyle; is tolerant, flexible, patient, and able to grow. An adopter who might not yet be ready can be too rigid or immature, have an incompatibility with his or her spouse, and have an indecisiveness about adoption. That wavering is a danger signal because it may result in only a partial acceptance of the child, with long-lasting implications for the emotional health of the child. Sometimes waiting, waiting, and more waiting will strengthen the desire. Sometimes waiting will extinguish the desire. Above all, you must be brutally honest with yourselves.

The American Fertility Society has some advice on making this decision.

> There are no set guidelines to determine who should or should not adopt. Signs suggesting indecision could include denial of your disappointment about infertility; persistent fantasies about what life might have been like with biological children; and a desire to keep the adoption a secret. Prospective parents may also have fears that an adoptive child won't measure up to family standards, and they may feel uncomfortable about the attitudes of a child's birth parents.[12]

If you have any of these concerns, seek out the advice of a counselor or clergy person before proceeding. Don't allow yourself to be driven by selfish personal desires and needs at the sacrifice of a child's physical, spiritual, and emotional well-being. If you aren't ready, you need to be honest with yourselves. A child needs to be unhesitatingly welcomed into a family. Perhaps time and prayer will strengthen your convictions. Give yourselves and that potential son or daughter all the time you need to make the right choice.

 **FIVE**

Adopting after Infertility

Well, you can always adopt." I cannot count the number of times I heard this expressed while my husband and I struggled with infertility. Although it was often spoken as a comfort, the words often angered me and led to subsequent confusion.

I was inexplicably angry at pregnant women—especially those who complained about its discomforts. Didn't they see what a blessing they had? I have actually had some women inform me that I was lucky because I didn't have to endure pregnancy and labor for part of my brood of children. Little did they know how much I longed for that experience.

I could relate to Rachel in the Old Testament, who was unable to bear Jacob's children. She was jealous of her sister, Leah, and her fertility. She cried to Jacob, "Give me children, or I'll die!" (Gen. 30:1). The pain of infertility feels like a kind of death—the death of hope, the death of regeneration. Each twenty-eight-day cycle that elapses without conception is a ride from hope to despair, from life to death. For the woman who has also suffered miscarriage, this pain is doubled.

Society's view of infertility only compounds the problem. It is often viewed as a sign or a judgment. A subsequent adoption says to the world that we have no control over our bloodlines or heredity.

For most of us, the information we do have about our own bloodlines is often sketchy and sometimes frightening. Most families have their share of inherited illness, either mental or physical. Yet it is sometimes viewed as unacceptable to adopt a child with a less than complete history. Are our current families much different? My father was born in Ireland, and I know little about his history because it is shrouded in the secrecy of various Irish rebellions. My maternal grandmother was from Lithuania, and her ancestors were often a people without their own country. My point is that I know little about my own background. Perhaps that is why adopting a child with an incomplete family history does not frighten me.

The issues of infertility and adoption are separate and distinct. Every woman cherishes her fertility and the potential to carry new life within her body. When that is not a possibility, a grieving process takes place that must be experienced entirely before adoption is considered.

It is a personal, private, terrible grief. Your body or your spouse's body, for whatever earthly reason or higher purpose, has failed you. Something you may have taken for granted and expected since childhood is no longer a possibility.

Patricia Irwin Johnston in her book *Adopting after Infertility* discusses six losses that accompany the infertility experience.

1. Loss of control;
2. Loss of individual genetic continuity;
3. Loss of a jointly conceived child;
4. Loss of the physical expectations of the pregnancy experience itself and of feeling the power to impregnate;

5. Loss of the emotional expectations about a shared pregnancy, birth, breast feeding experience; and
6. Loss of the opportunity to parent.[1]

Each of these losses must be dealt with individually.

Here is the best description I've found of the pain of infertility:

> Infertility is a prolonged shriek of pain that makes no sound. It is the woman who averts her eyes each time she passes a baby in a stroller, wells up at the sight of a diaper ad, goes numb when a friend announces that she's pregnant. It is the man who resents providing semen samples in plastic cups, dreads ingesting his wife with fertility drugs, longs for spontaneous sex.[2]

According to RESOLVE, a national support group for individuals dealing with infertility, 5.3 million people in the United States are infertile. Put another way, about one in six couples of childbearing age are thought to be infertile.[3]

Infertility has crept up on many of us who were preoccupied with other things. Planning careers and pursuing educational goals may have taken a woman's focus off her fertility. Many of us figured we could schedule our pregnancies like we mapped and scheduled our careers. While other goals may have been successfully attained, for the infertile it is a problem of the body not cooperating with the management plan. Unlike saving for a home or completing an educational degree, a baby can't always be scheduled, and continued fertility cannot always be controlled. Babies and children have their own timetable and their own part in God's plan.

If you are struggling with fertility issues, one of the first resources to turn to is RESOLVE. RESOLVE provides support, information, advocacy, and referrals for those experiencing infertility (see appendix A for the address and phone number). About 90 percent of the time doctors can find a physical cause for infertility. It may or may not be correctable. You may not even want to have the precise, scientific answer for your infertility.

It didn't take long for us to reach the "enough is enough" phase. After infertility, miscarriage, and minimal fertility testing, we surmised we could agonize over our biological lot or pursue adoption. Because it didn't matter to us how our children came to us, we cut short heroic measures of attaining fertility. It was too expensive and felt too much like we were trying to manipulate some plan other than what God was mapping out for us. We let go, and God blessed that trust in him.

You often hear this advice: Adopt a child and you'll get pregnant. Although this is what actually happened in our case, a figure your physician is likely to tell you is that five to eight percent of infertile couples eventually get pregnant whether or not they adopt. As previously discussed, this should not be your motivation to adopt. Such a tactic robs your adopted child of the unconditional love she deserves.

Enough Is Enough!

How will you know when enough is enough? Author Elaine Walker says, "Mourning what may never be is essential to becoming ready to accept what can. Adoption will take away the pain of being childless, but it will not remove the loss over being unable to procreate."[4] She offers these questions for your consideration:

1. Have you begun to lose energy for more infertility treatments? Do you dread your next doctor's appointment? Do you suspect that the treatment you're undergoing is futile and that other treatments are apt to be ineffective as well? Would it be a relief to stop trying

to get pregnant and put more energy into other aspects of your life?

2. Is having a child to love more important to you than how the child joins your family?

3. Are you finally at peace with other people giving birth rather than bursting into tears when one of your friends announces her pregnancy?

4. Have you grieved for the loss of your dream child? Do you feel you can now let go and begin dreaming of another child?[5]

If you are truly despairing over your infertility, you should wait until you have dealt with some of your disappointment before applying for adoption. Adoption is not a second-best choice. To be truly ready to adopt is to be able to say a resounding Yes! to adoption rather than a Well, if that's all I can get . . . The goal of all potential parents is parenthood, not necessarily pregnancy. If you are ready to adopt, there is probably a child somewhere, dreaming of having parents like you.

Can I Try to Do Both?

Many adoptive couples have one common regret: They did not act sooner to pursue adoption. After fertility treatments have dragged out over many years, combined with being on agency waiting lists for several years, some couples find that the total time of waiting for a child stretches well over a decade.

While coping with infertility is hard, it is also difficult for many to take the step into adoption. You should not adopt before you are ready to do so, but be aware of the years that are slipping by without your being able to love your own child. The saddest stories are those of couples who have left no stone unturned in their quest for fertility only to find that they are then too old to apply at most adoption agencies. They spent too much time pursuing a biological solution.

Agencies differ on their policies concerning pursuit of infertility treatment and adoption simultaneously. Some may require that you cease fertility treatment while in the adoption process. Most will require that your in-process adoption be put on hold should you become pregnant.

From a financial as well as an emotional perspective, you may not be able to pursue both options at once. Both are expensive and draining.

Some social workers may advise you that to feel fully committed to your adopted child, you should be prepared to be fully committed to the adoption process—not doing it as a stopgap measure. You need to follow the dictates of whichever agency you choose, as well as listening to the wisdom of your own heart. God works miracles all the time. Some of them are biological pregnancies. Some of them are adoptions.

All are wonderful.

 **SIX**

Can I Adopt the Child I Want?

You've probably heard it said, There's only one way to make a baby but many ways to make a family. I wish that everyone who wants a child could experience easy conception and a trouble-free pregnancy and be assured of a healthy birth child or children. Life isn't like that. Fortunately, other options exist for adults who want to build a life with children. Adoption and foster parenting are two routes to the joy of family. Within each of these categories, the variety is extensive.

There is much to encourage the childless in this quest. In her book *To Love a Child* author Marianne Takas says:

> You should know that the most basic core of your dream— to care for and nurture a child or children—is absolutely, unquestionably both possible and practical, without waiting, without scheming, and without spending money you can't afford. . . . To say that there is, right now, a child waiting for you would be an understatement. More accurately, there

are one or three or even several children waiting—as many as you have room for in your life and in your heart.[1]

If this is the case, why does adoption have the image of being a costly, drawn-out proposition? This has to do largely with the kinds of children readily available for adoption in our society today compared to the attitude that we will only accept a child perfectly matched to our family. Also, the misinformed notion that adoption should be as easy as filling out forms at an agency makes the reality seem worse than it is.

In the early days of adoption practice in this country, the typical adopting couple was usually white, infertile, and middle class and was usually seeking a healthy, white infant to adopt. In fact the custom of social workers was to try to match an available infant with parents having similar physical characteristics.

A few decades have passed, and how times have changed! Hard-to-place children (now called "special needs" children) are increasingly placed successfully. Adoption now crosses racial and ethnic lines. Older children or those with other special needs who were once destined to spend their lives in orphanages are now finding homes—some permanent, some in temporary foster care.

Adoption is becoming such an accepted, widespread practice that it is no longer the chief concern of adoptive parents to raise a child who looks just like them. Families are celebrating diversity and the differences that gave them an opportunity to be a family together.

Today a child in need of parenting may be any race or any age, may have physical or emotional difficulties, and may have and wish to maintain at least some form of relationship with parents, siblings, or other family members. Older child adoption, foster parenting, and child and family mentoring are now far more commonly needed than adoption of an infant. Yet while the needs of the children have changed dramatically, the focus of most adults hoping to parent has been much slower to change . . . the result is often sadly missed connections.[2]

If your goal is to build a family, you may need to focus more on what you have to offer a child and be more flexible in terms of what type of child you could parent. If you have a burning desire to parent, could you effectively parent a less-than-perfect child? If you can only accept the perfect child, you may have to pursue your options more aggressively or vigorously. With a broader perspective, opportunities abound for building a rich life with children.

Conversely, you shouldn't be discouraged if your goal is to adopt a healthy, same-race infant. You may have to be more creative, patient, and tenacious than in other adoptions, but don't give up.

Most adoptive parents can, in retrospect, see the sure hand of God guiding them to their children. They describe it in various ways. Pam Walsh of Wheaton, Illinois, says of her adoption, "We didn't exactly choose this type of adoption; it fell in our laps." Jill Bull says, "International adoption was God's decision, not ours." Many adoptive parents can identify the providence of God in their adoptions. Often details are arranged and needs are met in a supernatural way. For the Christian family, the experience can cement their faith.

Same-Race Infant Adoption

The face of adoption has changed dramatically over the last several decades. In the early days of adoption some couples were actually given a choice of selecting from two or more healthy babies. Children who came into the social welfare system handicapped, older, or mentally challenged were considered unadoptable and were left to languish in orphanages and more recently in foster care.

Today there are actually still more children to adopt than there are parents applying for adoption, but the waiting children aren't all healthy babies.

Since so many people want to adopt healthy, same-race infants, some agencies inform parents that they can expect to wait several years for placement. Some agencies allow the birth mother to choose the adoptive family, and the family history or résumé is placed in a pool with those of other waiting applicants. This process may decrease the waiting time.

In many states adoptive parents can bypass agency requirements and waiting lists by pursuing an independent adoption. Many couples have found the child of their dreams in less than a year using this method. In 1992 37.5 percent of all adoptions were either through a private agency or were independent adoptions.

Be aware that independent placement, while legal in most states, is illegal in some. As of the mid-1990s independent placements were not permitted in Connecticut, Delaware, Massachusetts, Michigan, or North Dakota. You will need to be very clear on what is permitted in your state. The value of competent legal counsel cannot be understated.

The problem in same-race, healthy infant adoption is not a lack of resources. There are a few thousand adoption agencies in the United States plus hundreds of lawyers and other intermediaries who are eager to help you. The problem is choosing a method to locate a birth mother and being persistent and patient.

International Adoption

In 1993 there were 7,348 adoptions of children who were born overseas, according to the latest statistics available from the United States Immigration and Naturalization Service. Although this number is encouraging for adoptive parents, the number is down from the 1987 figure of 10,097 overseas adoptions, the highest annual total ever.

Of these adoptions, 1,522 were from Romania and the former Soviet Union; 3,163 were from Asia; 59 from Africa; 97 from Mexico; 158 from the Caribbean; 878 from Central America; and 1,471 from South America. As you gather information and make a decision about an international adoption, it is helpful to know which countries are allowing adoptions and how many children are placed each year. This can help you decide where you are most likely to succeed in the shortest period of time.

While the application and processing of an international adoption may be a bit more complicated than for a domestic adoption, you are probably less likely to run into legal problems once the child is on American soil. A child would not be cleared from a foreign country if the consent of the birth parents was still at issue. Many couples choose international adoption because of this fact, especially in light of recent adoption cases gone awry.

International adoption will change your family for generations. If you become an interracial family, you will get a lot of public attention because your child will not look like you. I cannot count the number of times I have heard the questions, "Where did you get that baby?" or "How much did she cost?" An adoptive family with a child from Vietnam answers rude questions this way: "She isn't supposed to look like us. She's supposed to look like her!"[3]

When you adopt a child from another culture, you should be willing to learn about the other culture to help keep those ties alive for your child. This may mean learning to cook a new cuisine or to attend church with people who look like your child.

If you can envision your family not as white or brown or Asian but as a family of God, you will make an ideal international adoptive family.

Special Needs Adoption

All over the world there are special children waiting for families. Some are disabled or hearing- or sight-impaired. Some were born with birth defects. Others are healthy but are older or belong to sibling groups.

The term "special needs" is a broad one and refers to "any characteristic that makes it hard for a child to find a home: age, membership in a sibling group, race or ethnic background, or a physical, mental or emotional disability. The greater the special need, the more flexible the requirements for adoption are apt to be."[4]

Public agencies have a catalog of waiting children. When we visited our first adoption agency, I thought this was bizarre. The catalog had photographs and descriptions of waiting children. Upon reflection, I realized this is the agency's way of recruiting potential families. Because so many children wait, such a listing shared by many agencies is the best way to spread the news of the availability of the children.

For some families, a type of special need fits in well with their abilities and expectations. A husband who was raised with a Down's syndrome brother, for example, would be an ideal adoptive parent for this type of child. Or a family who has experienced epilepsy with one of its members may find this condition unexceptional. On the other hand, there may be conditions or handicaps that you truly cannot deal with. You need to be honest about what fits in with your capabilities. The reality of day-to-day life with a handicapped child can take you far from the feelings of compassion you may have had when considering this choice.

Some special needs children find permanent homes through their foster placements. Experts agree that these families make the easiest adjustment. They have had the time to get to know each other and experience real life together before considering adoption. When such a child becomes available for adoption, many foster parents take the opportunity to finalize an adoption.

Older Children

Most agencies consider children about twelve or over to fall in the special needs category because adoptive parents are generally interested in younger children. Older children may have had difficult life experiences, such as abuse or neglect. Their entry into a home involves a major adjustment for them as well as for their adoptive family. Some liken the process more to a marriage than an adoption.

These children go through a distinct grieving process. Unlike an infant, they come to your home with memories, experiences, and preferences. Their personalities are most likely already formed, and it may take time for a real love to grow between you.

These children enter foster care and become available for adoption for a variety of reasons. Some are surrendered by their parents, who have difficulty caring for them. Others are removed from homes by court order for neglect or abuse.

In adopting an older child, it is most of all important to be flexible. Can you accept that this child has a past and that it will take time to gain his love and respect? Can you love a child who may not immediately love you back? Can you endure the inevitable testing period that will ensue as the older child seeks to establish his place in your home?

For many, such as an older childless couple, the adoption of an older child is ideal. The mother of forty-five or fifty may not have the interest or energy to keep up with a toddler but would have the right mixture of maturity and flexibility to effectively parent a twelve-year-old.[5]

Sibling Groups

A sibling group may consist of two or more children of varying ages, perhaps even teenagers. They generally have a strong family bond with one another, and the oldest child may have assumed a parental role for the group. Authors Wirth and Worden caution, "These children have survived by strongly bonding with one another and treating outsiders with suspicion. (The adoptive parents will be outsiders for a very long time—maybe always.)"[6] They know each other well and will be more secure if they can be placed together. Agencies recognize this fact and will look for families who will adopt all of the children together.

The oldest child's assumed parental role is not easily changed. The adoptive parents have to consistently prove that they can do a better job of parenting before the oldest sibling will allow the sibling group to trust a new family.

It is believed that the best family to adopt a sibling group is either childless or already large, that is, having four or more children. The most difficult placement of siblings is in a family that has one or two birth children, which sets up an "us against them" scenario.[7] Consider first the needs of your current family before taking on this responsibility. If you can afford it financially and emotionally, and you know you want to raise a large family, this may be the route for you to explore.

As with other special needs children, sometimes sibling groups are adopted by their foster families. Having spent a period of time together and already feeling like a family, this can be a smooth adjustment for everyone.

Minority-Race or Mixed-Race Children

Agencies have traditionally preferred to place children in same-race families, but there are insufficient minority families for all of the minority children awaiting adoption in this country. Recently, new policy guidelines have been promulgated by the U.S. Department of Health and Human Services regarding multi-ethnic placements.

Agencies that receive federal funding for foster care or adoption services will no longer be permitted to follow a placement preference for same-race or same-ethnicity matches. The rules provide, however, that on a case-by-case basis agencies *may* examine prospective parents' capacity to meet a child's psychological needs as they relate to the child's racial, ethnic, or cultural background.

A recent *Time* article highlighted prejudice against transracial placements:

> Of the roughly 440,000 children who currently languish in America's foster-care system, 20,000 are available for adoption, most of them older children between the ages of six and twelve. Among the adoptable children, 44% are white and 43% are black. But 67% of all families waiting to adopt are white, and many of them are eager to take a black child.[8]

Why aren't these waiting families matched with the available children, regardless of their color? Is it the prejudice of adoptive families or of social workers? Parents and children are missing an opportunity.

African American children waiting for placement cover a wide range of ages and include healthy infants. According to the National Adoption Center, the greatest number of waiting black children are boys of school age.

In an ideal world, children would be perfectly matched with parents of their own racial or ethnic backgrounds. But this is not reality. I believe that children should be raised by parents who love, understand, and accept them, no matter what their color or background. If children know that they are truly loved and wanted, they will be able to face life with confidence, no matter how many colors or nationalities are represented in their family.

The National Adoption Information Clearinghouse advises parents with a transracial or transcultural family to:

1. Become intensely invested in parenting;
2. Tolerate no racially or ethnically biased remarks;
3. Surround yourselves with supportive family and friends;
4. Celebrate all cultures;
5. Talk about race and culture;
6. Expose your child to a variety of experiences so that he or she develops physical and intellectual skills that build self-esteem; and
7. Take your child to places where most of the people present are from his or her race or ethnic group.[9]

Physically, Mentally, or Emotionally Challenged Children

Bill Holton tells the moving story of a blind couple who waited for many years to adopt a child. A partially sight-impaired one-year-old from Korea was placed with them through Holt International Children's Services. It was an answer to prayer for these childhood sweethearts, both blind from birth. They reasoned that lots of blind biological parents are raising sighted children and doing a good job of it: "After all, it's not what you can or can't see that makes you a good parent, it's what you teach your child about love and life and living in the world."[10]

A physically challenged child may have any number of disabilities, such as AIDS, Down's syndrome, fetal alcohol syndrome, autism, attention deficit disorder, spina bifida, or epilepsy, to name just a few. The listings of available children with physical challenges seem endless.

It is estimated that more than a million people in the United States are considering adoption at any given time. Most are dreaming of the perfect child who looks like them.

Yet to wait a childless lifetime for a dream that may not be fulfilled seems empty compared to the love that could be in your midst by adopting a special needs child.

Is Special Needs Adoption for You?

How can you know if such a child is for your family? Authors Wirth and Worden say that successful parents of children with special needs share certain characteristics. Specifically,

> They have a highly realistic notion of what children are like. They work to help a child develop his or her potential, but their egos do not depend on the success of perfect children. They are flexible. They have a great deal of love to give, but understand that they must meet their own needs in order to meet the needs of their children.[11]

According to Elaine Walker, your self-assessment should include your honest answers to the following:

- Are you flexible? Do you have a well-developed sense of humor?
- Do you have a lot of emotional and physical energy?
- Do you have the financial resources to meet your child's needs? Can you afford to pay for all of the expenses that are not covered by health insurance or adoption subsidies?
- Do you have experience with children?
- Can you accept a child just as he is? Or do you need a lot of feedback and a sense of achievement?
- Do you need the approval and acceptance of your peers? Will it bother you if your child "gets into trouble"? If her appearance is unusual or discomforting?
- Are you able to work well with outside support, such as counselors, psychologists, social workers, etc.?
- Are you able to cope with chronic illness? Do you stay calm during emergencies?

- Are you able to cope with behavioral and bonding problems such as lying, stealing, skipping school, and hurting others?
- Are you willing to learn all about your child's specific needs? Will you work to get him or her the appropriate services?[12]

The National Adoption Center is a resource through which children waiting to be adopted are made known to families interested in adopting them (see appendix A for the address and phone number). This is not an adoption agency but can provide extensive information to you and will work with agencies around the country who have custody of waiting children. If you are considering special needs adoption, get this organization's information.

Most agencies and social workers are eager to work with parents who are interested in special needs adoption. You don't have to be wealthy, own a home, or be experienced parents. Many single parents have adopted special needs children.

The experts at Adoptive Families of America (AFA) caution that adoption of a special needs child is not for everyone. Those who are successful genuinely like children and enjoy the challenges of parenting. They also:

- Can handle change and stress
- Accept a child with a past and the surprises that brings
- Have good emotional survival skills
- Encourage open communication
- Can cope with rejection and anger without personalizing it
- Realize that not all problems can be overcome
- Advocate for their children when necessary
- Express love and trust
- Have a sense of humor[13]

Can I Adopt the Child I Want?

Financial Assistance for Special Needs

Agencies vary in costs, but the fees for special needs adoptions are moderate. For public agencies, there may be no fees. In fact you may qualify for adoptive assistance. Many private companies also offer adoption benefits, including those for legal expenses, adoption fees, and medical expenses.

Financial assistance from public agencies may come from federal or state programs. It can include adoption fees, court costs, attorney fees, and other expenses. Many state subsidy programs are determined by the child's needs and not the financial welfare of the adopting parents. The adoptive family's income does not affect a child's eligibility for a subsidy but may affect the amount. Subsidies may include support payments, Medicaid (federal health insurance benefit), and social services under the Social Security Act. Your social worker will give you complete information about all available assistance.

The Adoption Assistance and Child Welfare Act of 1980 provides federal funds for the adoption of children when these criteria are met:

1. The child meets the state definition of special needs. Each state has its own criteria but generally requires that the children be over two when adopted; are adopted as part of a sibling group; are at high risk of developing disabilities (such as the drug-exposed); or have a mental, physical, or emotional disability.
2. The adoptive family qualifies for AFDC (Aid to Families with Dependent Children) or SSI (Supplemental Security Income).

An agency will usually give you a written Adoption Assistance Agreement before the adoption is finalized. If you are not satisfied with this agreement, see what items are nego-

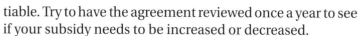

tiable. Try to have the agreement reviewed once a year to see if your subsidy needs to be increased or decreased.

Once a child is an adult, all benefits to the adoptive parents cease. If the child is one who is never expected to live independently, this could be an important factor in your overall adoption plans.

Adoptive Families of America, the American Public Welfare Association, the National Adoption Information Clearinghouse, and the North American Council on Adoptable Children offer further information on subsidies for adoptions. If you are considering special needs adoption, write to each of these groups requesting their subsidy publications (see appendix A for addresses).

Foster Parenting

The foster care system in our country is intended to be a temporary situation for children while permanent plans are being made. It is hoped that children in foster care "can either return home or, if this is not possible, be adopted. In reality, however, foster care is temporary for less than a third of the children who come under the system."[14] Put another way, two-thirds of the children who come into foster care will remain there, in a state of limbo, until they are grown.

Families choose to foster parent for a variety of reasons. Some see it as a ministry to help uprooted children. Some provide foster care to new infants for the short period of time during which they are cleared for adoption. Some do it to earn extra income. Whatever the reason, foster parents provide an invaluable service and sometimes end up adopting the children they care for.

Recognizing and trying to encourage this trend, some agencies have a fost-adopt program, which is a mixture of foster care and adoption. Some call these programs "legal risk" adoption programs. If a child comes into the system and it seems likely that the child will be freed for adoption, the child will be placed with a family who has indicated their interest in fost-adoption. When and if the child becomes legally available, these foster parents are given the first opportunity to adopt the child.

While this does not guarantee that a family will be able to adopt, it does provide a trial period for everyone involved and allows the foster family to have precedence over other potential adoptive families. It can be an emotional roller coaster for the foster parents, in part because the birth parents have the right to visit their child until their legal rights are terminated. This would strain the hopes of the foster parents, who would always wonder if they were one visit away from losing their foster child.

In fost-adopt, or legal risk, there are varying degrees of risk. If one of these placements interests you, get as much information as you can so you can evaluate whether the risk is low or high. Find out what you can about the birth family. Have they been involved with the child or in contact with the child at all? Keep in mind that if you do pursue the adoption of a foster child, you may be eligible for subsidies if the child meets the guidelines.

An excellent source of information for those interested in any type of foster parenting is the National Foster Parent Association. It is a national support organization offering referrals to local groups, an excellent newsletter, and other information services (see appendix A for the address and phone number).

Mentoring

If your goal is to make a difference in a child's life, opportunities abound in your own community. Neighborhood children often cherish the added attention of a neighbor who takes the time to listen to them. Schools are desperately in need of volunteers, given the number of two-wage-earner families their students represent. The YMCA or YWCA may be good starting points for exploring this area, as well as Boys Clubs and Girls Clubs, Scouts, and Big Brother or Big Sister programs. Other places where you could be involved include the 4-H Club, Junior Achievement, or the United Way. Finally, don't neglect the closest opportunity for many of us—our church. Sunday school departments and youth groups are woefully understaffed.

A mentor, according to a recent Capital Cities/ABC Children First media campaign, is any caring adult who makes an active, positive contribution to the life of a child who is not his or her own. It's a friend, a guide, a coach. It doesn't take a lot of money or qualifications, just a little time. You can change two lives through mentoring—a child's and yours.

 SEVEN

An Adoption Overview

esearching adoption can be overwhelming. There is much to learn and consider and critical decisions to be made. They are best made with deep prayer, trust, and faith and with a solid basis of knowledge.

One attorney delineates twelve different routes that may be pursued leading toward adoption.

- Private adoption agencies performing domestic adoptions (American-born children)
- Private adoption agencies performing international adoptions (foreign-born children)
- Private adoption agencies located outside your home state but able to perform domestic and international adoptions within your state or in the state where the agency is located
- Public/county adoption agencies
- The foster parent shortcut
- Independent domestic adoption (American-born children)
- Independent international adoption (foreign-born children)
- Independent adoption initiated by attorneys located

outside your home state, but able to assist in domestic
and international adoptions by working with an attorney or agency within your home state
- Independent nonresident adoption which allows adoptive parents to adopt a child in the state where the child
is born, even if independent adoption is not permitted
in the adoptive parents' home state
- Identified adoptions
- Facilitator-initiated adoptions
- Special needs adoption registries.[1]

Many of these methods have overlapping characteristics but
each will be discussed.

Domestic Agency Adoptions

Most people who think of adoption think of the traditional
agency adoption. An agency acts as an intermediary or
ombudsman between adoptive parents and birth parents.

There are public and private agencies. Public agencies are
subsidiaries or affiliates of the state or local government and
are operated with government funds. The children available
through a public agency are usually those in the state's foster care system. Public agencies handle predominantly special needs adoptions, such as those of older children, fully
or partially disabled children, children who have been
abused or neglected, sibling groups, or minority or racially
mixed children.

Private agencies are typically nonprofit corporations (although there are some for-profit private agencies as well),
many of which are affiliated with churches or religious
denominations. Just because an agency has a denominational tag to its name, such as Evangelical Child and Family
Services or Catholic Charities, don't assume that you must
be a member of that particular denomination to use the

agency. A few agencies require a specific denominational affiliation, but most do not.

If you receive a perfunctory response to your first call to an agency, don't be discouraged. Can you imagine how many calls they get? Once you get established with an agency, you will feel as comfortable as calling an old friend.

Advantages and Disadvantages

For a birth mother, an agency adoption can provide several advantages. Of primary importance to many birth mothers is the screening of adoptive parents performed by the agency to ensure the child will be placed in a good home. This professional scrutiny by an agency can be a great source of comfort to the birth mother.

Many agencies are allowing birth mothers to exercise a greater degree of control in the selection of adoptive parents. A mother may be presented with the résumés of several couples and given the opportunity to select between the couples and meet with them if she desires.

The birth mother may maintain her anonymity if she wishes, because the agency will act as an intermediary. On the other hand, if she wants contact and communication with the adoptive parents, an agency can facilitate this as well.

An advantage to both the birth mother and the adoptive parents is the counseling provided by an agency. Tremendous counseling and education of adoptive parents occurs during the home study. By its conclusion, the adoptive parents should feel ready to assume their new parental responsibilities without reservation. Most agencies will also counsel the birth mother for several sessions before accepting the surrender of her child. This gives her the opportunity to explore all her options and feelings prior to placement and to freely change her mind if that is her choice. Where possible, the birth father should be a part of the counseling. One criticism of non-agency adoption is that the birth mother may receive inadequate counseling, making her less certain of her decision.

There are also disadvantages to agency adoption. Many adoptive parents are discouraged by the seemingly interminable waiting, typically anywhere from five to eight years. An agency may also have age limitations that would preclude the successful application of a couple over forty. Some agencies are not able or willing to help with the birth mother's medical bills.

Placement

In a private or public agency infant adoption, the birth mother signs documents to surrender to the agency her legal rights to her child, giving the agency legal guardianship. The agency then places the child in the custody of waiting adoptive parents. These parents usually have successfully completed a home study screening process, but the agency involvement does not conclude directly after placement. Typically there is a waiting period of six to twelve months during which the agency makes post-placement visits to determine the success of the placement. During that time frame, the child is still legally tied to the agency, with temporary custody granted to the adoptive parents. After this period the agency then legally relinquishes to the adoptive parents its rights to the child, and the adoption may be finalized in a civil court.

In a traditional agency adoption, the child *may* spend some period of time in a foster home, where she will stay until all the legal papers are in order. This can take a few days to several months. When the birth parents have signed the surrenders and the child is legally free for adoption, the adoptive parents are allowed to take the child home.

Some agencies are experimenting with "direct placements." In this scenario, the child goes directly home from the hospital to the home of the adoptive parents without any waiting time spent in foster care. This practice began as a result of birth mothers' dissatisfaction with the foster care system. They wanted their babies to be able to bond with their new families as soon as possible.

Adoptive parents should know that this practice is done at some risk, as the birth mother may change her mind before giving her final consent, or other legal problems might arise that would cause the child to be removed from the adoptive home. This can be a heartbreaking experience for all involved. Yet direct placement is employed successfully when the birth parents have been adequately counseled and are confident of their decision.

Choosing an Agency

The optimal way to select an agency is by word of mouth. It is amazing to me that couples will spend months researching the strengths and weaknesses of different computers before purchasing one but will call any ad in the phone book for an adoption agency because it "looked like a nice agency."

As incongruous as it may seem, as a potential adoptive family, you are a consumer. In seeking out adoption professionals to assist you, you need to analyze their strengths and weaknesses from a consumer's viewpoint. Private agencies have been known to go out of business, sometimes after receiving huge up-front fees from their clients. Your first duty should be to check that any agency you deal with is licensed by the state adoptive regulatory agency, but even that may not be sufficient. The recommendation of adoptive parents or other adoption professionals who have first-hand experience with the agency or professional you are looking at is the best way to choose.

Talk to other couples who have adopted. If you don't know any, ask for referrals from your church or from an agency or join an adoptive support group. Most adoptive families are delighted to talk about their experiences, and they are the best source of information about the strengths and weaknesses of various agencies.

Costs

Costs for a public agency adoption may range from nothing to a few thousand dollars. A private agency's costs, whether for-profit or not-for-profit, range from ten thousand dollars to twenty thousand dollars or more.

Unfortunately, agencies are subject to the same consumer challenges as any other business entity. The best advice is for the buyer to beware. In doing your research, you will be able to determine whether your agency's fees are above or below the norm. If the fees are out of line, you may accept them, decline them and choose another agency, or ask the agency to explain the reason for the high amount.

Author Nancy Reynolds's advice is to ask an agency to explain its fee structure. This can provide important information.

> Perhaps the fee is higher because more services are provided. Perhaps the agency is supporting an orphanage in Latin America or subsidizing adoption fees for adopters with low incomes. Perhaps the fee is higher because the agency is a for-profit business and is advertising on television and radio to locate birth mothers. Perhaps the fee is higher because illegal payments are being made to birth mothers to persuade them to place their children with that agency.[2]

Whatever the reason, you *want* to know. Being informed is the best way to choose an agency that meets your needs.

For-Profit Agencies

A healthy infant adoption through a traditional agency may take six years or more. Many agencies are quoting a waiting time of six to eight years. Some for-profit agencies, which aggressively recruit birth mothers and charge commensurately higher fees, can secure an adoption in a year or so. The adoption of an older child or one with special needs may take less than a year. The better for-profit agencies offer counseling to birth mothers, but some do not.

Many nonprofit agencies are criticized for being too passive. They wait to be approached by pregnant women who want to make an adoption plan rather than seeking them out. The busy for-profit agencies that locate a lot of children do an aggressive job of seeking out birth mothers. They may place extensive advertisements and have many contacts in the community by which referrals are made. This approach is not taken by most nonprofit agencies because they tend to view their work as a ministry rather than a business. As an adoptive parent, you can choose which approach is the most comfortable for you.

International Agency Adoptions

International adoptions are becoming increasingly popular given the difficulty in locating a baby to adopt in the United States. The minimum age for adoptive parents is usually twenty-five, and a marriage of two to five years' duration is usually required. The upper age limit is usually around forty, but countries may differ. International adoption takes an average time of from one to three years.

International adoption programs, particularly those from Eastern Europe, change constantly. Any specific information provided in this book would likely be out of date by publication. However, the parent group International Concerns Committee for Children constantly updates international adoption information and can provide the very latest information about what programs are available and what agencies to contact. Their publication is *The Report on Foreign Adoption* (see appendix A for the address and phone number).

The demography of international adoption changes rather frequently. Some countries will allow adoptions, then abruptly stop. Other countries have been a reliable, consistent source of adoptable children.

One agency may offer international programs for several countries or may specialize in one country or geographic area of the world. Each program is likely to have different requirements, so you will want to get an overview of which programs you may qualify for before settling on a country. For example, some countries have age requirements and require that no other children are in the household. Some agencies are licensed to work with only certain states. If you don't meet the requirements for one agency, make sure you know why, then inquire at several others.

Perhaps, like us, you will know instinctively which country appeals to you. Maybe you have met children from this country and fallen in love with them. We have always loved Asian faces. One of my husband's fondest memories from the military is seeing Asian children and their beautiful faces. When we considered international adoption, we knew immediately where we were headed.

Many couples are interested in adopting from Eastern Europe because they think that a child from there will be less "foreign" looking. International adoption experts Wirth and Worden say these "children may not look like your expectations, since about half are from Gypsy families and have dark skin and eyes." In addition, you may encounter other problems with these children because of the care they receive while still overseas. "Many children who have been in crowded orphanages may need a great deal of special attention to overcome the impact of years of institutionalization."[3] As with any adoption, a committed, knowledgeable, and loving parent can deal with any situation.

Why International?

People choose international adoption for different reasons. "While some prospective Caucasian parents (the majority of U.S. adopters) chose intercountry adoption because they value its intercultural nature," comments Joan D. Ramos, M.S.W., "others may choose it as a means to avoid the openness prevalent in today's domestic placements."[4]

With many birth mothers wishing to maintain contact with their children, adoptive parents who cannot accept this are seeking children from other lands. A related factor for our family was the lessened likelihood of some legal glitch in the adoption process. We reasoned that once a child was released from Korea for adoption, there was little chance her birth parents would come to the United States to try to nullify the consent proceeding. Plus, the social situation in Korea tends to make birth parents more confident of their decision. A child born out of wedlock is shunned by society and places a large burden on the mother's family.

Families engage in a dramatically different preparation in considering international adoption. They face emotional and cultural questions that typically do not arise in healthy, same-race adoptions. Total strangers will comment on your family. You will be a walking advertisement for adoption. It becomes even more important for you to examine your hearts as well as the attitudes of extended family members.

Our experience with international adoption was extremely educational. This is typical and necessary. Couples in the international adoption process will spend a great deal of time being counseled on how to deal with cultural differences and their inherent potential problems.

The Process

I recommend that you not attempt an international adoption independently. Some couples have been successful but subjected themselves to legally risky and financially dangerous situations. You may have heard of a great connection in some country but find that after you have funneled lots of your money into that connection you have no guarantee that you will get a child. An agency that handles international adoptions can be verified, references can be checked, and you can proceed with more confidence.

Those who choose to pursue an international adoption directly may do so "because they want a child of a particular nationality and there is no agency placing those children. Others have family or friends who make a connection for them. Still others feel that they want to do the adoption themselves—and that includes finding their own child abroad," says Lois Gilman.[5] These do-it-yourself adoptions are popular in Columbia, where the social-service system is well organized for parents seeking independent adoption.

In many international situations, two agencies are involved—one in the United States and one in the country of the child's birth. Some countries will allow you to adopt without an intermediary agency, but all require a home study. This is actually a United States Immigration and Naturalization Service requirement: All people who bring a child into this country from another land must submit to a home study, which includes a criminal background check.

Once the local agency approves the parents, if there is a foreign agency, it must also approve them. Some agencies may require the adopting parents to travel to the foreign agency to pick up the child. Other agencies will arrange to have the child escorted to her new home.

Prior to coming to the United States for adoption, a foreign-born child must clear the United States Immigration and Naturalization Service (INS). A petition, along with supporting documents, is filed by the adopting parents asking that the child be eligible for an entry visa and asserting that the child is coming to the United States to be adopted. To speed this process, you may actually be able to file this petition before a specific child has been identified for you. In this instance, the adoptive parents file an Orphan Petition stating their intent. When a child is later identified, this petition will expedite the process of gaining permission for the child to leave the foreign country and enter the United States. If your agency has experience in dealing with international adoption, it will generally guide you in filing these petitions.

Your child will need a passport. If you are traveling to meet your child in her country, you will need a passport as well. Your agency will most likely make arrangements for the child's passport. You may apply for yours at a regional passport agency of the United States Department of State, at federal or state courts, or at some United States Post Offices. If you know you will be traveling, apply early, as they take several weeks to process.

On arrival your child will be classified as an alien, not as a citizen. Until you file further papers to apply for citizenship, she will have an alien registration card.

While some additional paperwork might be required for an international adoption, it is not any more intimidating or difficult than a domestic adoption. You should, however, make sure your attorney is familiar with and has experience with the peculiarities of international adoption. A misfiled paper or erroneously supplied legal information can cause interminable delays and perhaps irrevocable problems.

The booklet *The Immigration of Adopted and Prospective Adoptive Children*, available from the Immigration and Naturalization Service, will answer any further questions you may have about your child's entry into the United States (see appendix A for the address).

Costs

A typical international adoption can cost from five thousand dollars to sixteen thousand dollars and varies by agency and country. Some agencies use a sliding scale. Most have a flat fee. This does not include the cost of travel, if required.

Expenses are more extensive with an international adoption than a domestic adoption, including home study fees, legal fees, payment to child care institutions or foster care, medical care for the child, intercountry telecommunications, and documentation and translation, not to mention travel and lodging. One author notes:

> Often there will be a "program fee" that ostensibly goes to pay for social work and other services involved in the case. Across the board, the area of greatest variability seems to be the "in-country fee" that usually constitutes a direct payment to the facilitator who arranges the adoption.[6]

Your Child

While most parents will have a child's gender in mind when they begin to consider adoption, the more flexible you remain the quicker you may receive a referral. Authors Wirth and Worden observe, "More parents request girls than boys. Apparently more people believe that a foreign adopted girl will be better accepted than a boy. People who will accept a boy are likely to get a boy and get him sooner than those who insist on a girl."[7] As typical of the misinformation involved in adoption, we believed just the opposite and requested a girl, thinking she would arrive quicker. She arrived when God planned for her to arrive and we were very pleased.

The major concern of international adoptive parents should be the health of the child. Before a visa is issued for the child's travel, foreign-born children should undergo AIDS screening and hepatitis screening. This testing provides some assurance of health status. In addition, when you first receive your referral, you should get some medical information from your agency and later some actual medical records. It is a good idea to have your family physician look at these documents to alert you to anything unusual.

Some of the more common medical problems such as ear infections, sores, scabies, lice, or other parasites are easily correctable. Depending on the home country, the child may be of lower birth weight than that of children in the United States. This may or may not be a concern. Again, the child's whole health history should be discussed with your physician.

Private, or Independent, Adoption

In a private, or independent, adoption, adoptive parents or their intermediaries—such as doctors, lawyers, or adoption facilitators—locate babies directly and make arrangements with the birth mother without an agency serving as an intermediary. Sometimes this type of adoption is called a "direct placement." In this arrangement, a child is placed with adoptive parents immediately after birth. Consents are executed after the child has begun living in the adoptive home, so there is the risk that consents will not be forthcoming. One way to circumvent the risk is to have the child remain in the hospital until the consents are executed. With proper consents in hand, the adoptive couple can then take the baby home with greater confidence. Private adoptions are legal in all but a few states but are severely restricted in some.

Independent adoptions are popular. It is estimated that two-thirds of infant adoptions in the United States are carried out independently.[8] In trying to square these figures with the numbers from the National Adoption Information Clearinghouse, I believe this two-thirds refers to the 47,627 (or 37.5 percent) of the total adoptions in 1992 that were designated as being through a private agency or independent adoption.

Advantages and Disadvantages

The speed of independent adoption is one of its appeals. Researchers of private adoption recently concluded that "all but 2 of 105 infants had been placed in their adoptive homes within a year of their parents' starting to look."[9] A private or independent adoption can take as little as a few months or as long as a few years.

Most people choose this kind of adoption not because they have been rejected by an agency, but rather because they believe it is the most desirable way for them to build their family. In independent adoption, the adoptive parents are not subject to many of the requirements of adoption agencies, such as age restrictions, marital history, proof of infertility, or number of children. Even in private adoptions, however, the state may require some form of home study. This could be a comprehensive home study or a cursory meeting with county officials. These procedures vary widely from state to state and even within local jurisdictions.

Independent adoptions are popular with birth mothers who do not want to be subject to agency evaluation and counseling. A mother may feel that the agency workers will pass judgment on her, or she may have been turned off by an agency's approach. Likewise, she may also determine the amount of contact she is to have with the child and the adoptive parents, both before and after the birth of the child.

The birth mother may select the adoptive parents herself or may rely on the intermediary's judgment. She may or may not meet with the adoptive parents and play an active role in the adoption. One author said, "If the birth mother has her heart set on a Roman Catholic, non-drinking, harpsichord playing vegetarian couple, chances are the agencies and lawyers will do all they can to accommodate her wishes."[10]

States disallowing independent adoptions have the lowest rates of adoptions per capita. This may be because birth mothers desire the assurance of having had input in the adoption process. If a birth mother is not able to structure the adoption to suit her needs, she may not place the child. If she can exercise some control over her adoption plan, she is more likely to be at peace with her decision.

Attorney Stanley Michelman, who has helped hundreds of parents adopt, says this about the private adoption experience:

> In my experience, fewer changes of heart occur with independent adoption because the birth mother is more likely to be satisfied with her decision, especially since she knows something about her child's placement and has actively participated in planning her child's future. An adoption lawyer's goal is not simply to get an adoption done. An experienced lawyer will always attempt to weed out birth parents who are unsure. No one wants to be involved in a contested adoption.[11]

A birth mother may run the risk, however, of being unduly influenced by a facilitator who is less than scrupulous. I cannot stress enough how important it is to work with an ethical, principled attorney with knowledge, proven experience, and expertise in adoption law. To locate a qualified lawyer, confer with adoptive support groups and other adoptive parents and consult the directory in appendix B.

Another downside of independent adoption is that a birth mother may need counseling and may not get it. Much more attention would be focused on her decision-making process if she were to deal with an agency that could provide her with extensive guidance and counsel. But it is always possible, and desirable, to arrange for this counseling in an independent adoption as well.

Interstate Adoptions

An often overlooked adoption possibility is to seek a birth mother in another state and to pursue a nonresident independent adoption. Some adoptive parents feel that a child who comes from a distant state will have a better chance for a fresh start. Or they may have learned of the availability of a child in another location. Although this is permitted in most states, policies and procedures will vary, and you must have a legal counsel who is familiar with this arrangement.

If you are pursuing an independent adoption in another state, you will need to comply with the laws of both states. The Interstate Compact on the Placement of Children prohibits the transfer of a child from one state to another unless the appropriate public agency in the state where the child is to be received first approves of the arrangements. The sending agency or private attorney must send to the Compact administrator in the receiving state a notice that contains identifying information about the child, the birth parents, and the adoptive parents; a statement as to why the child is being sent; and evidence that this placement is authorized. Many lawyers are not knowledgeable about the Interstate Compact. Adoptive parents who do not comply with its provisions may be subject to criminal prosecution and may jeopardize the placement of their child.

Advertising

Arty Elgart, founder of one of the most successful private adoption agencies, Golden Cradle, believes that it pays to advertise. Some parents are put off by this and feel that it is less than ethical. In some states it is illegal. But where it is in compliance with the law, it can be an enormously effective way to locate birth mothers.

Concerning the founding of his adoption agency Mr. Elgart says:

> I concentrated on creating and placing ads that would reach an audience of birth mothers. The small personal notices I began with were soon replaced by larger ads which I then

placed in a wider range of neighborhood newspapers and magazines. . . . Before long, *Pregnant? Call Collect In Confidence*, in bold black-and-yellow lettering, began appearing on benches, in buses and taxicabs, across railroad trestles, on bumper stickers, even on Burger King tray liners!

The results for Golden Cradle were phenomenal. Elgart answers his detractors as follows: "Golden Cradle has been accused of using its ads to get babies. My answer to that is 'Yes—especially the babies who might otherwise be abused or abandoned.'"[12]

Costs

Costs vary widely. Adoptive parents are paying for the lawyer's fee as well as possibly for the expenses of the birth mother. In most states, adoptive parents are allowed to pay the medical expenses of the birth mother but they are forbidden from attaching any conditions to the payments. Some states permit the payment of living expenses for the birth mother until the birth of the child. In the states where any of these payments are allowed, the adopting parents must also file an accounting report with the court, which is signed under oath.

Some prospective parents sign a guarantee to the health care providers that they will pay the medical expenses of the birth mother. This does not guarantee, however, that the birth mother will place her child. If she changes her mind, the adoptive parents are still bound by the guarantee to meet her expenses. For those of us who err on the side of caution, as of this writing there are two insurance companies that will cover most expenses you would incur after making a commitment to a birth mother and the adoption fails: housing and living expenses, medical expenses, and adoption-related travel expenses. No legal costs are included. The insurance would be payable if the birth mother miscarries, the baby dies before consents are signed, or if the birth mother decides to parent the child herself. Of course, if the adoption goes ahead, adoptive parents would assume these expenses to the extent allowed. The premiums are hefty (between $1,500 to $2,500), but if you are interested in this type of coverage, ask your insurance agent to help you locate it through either Chubb and Sons or Lloyds of London.

More on Nontraditional Approaches

Closely related to independent adoption is something called "designated" or "identified" adoption. Using this method, adoptive parents can locate a birth mother themselves and put the adoption together. This gives adoptive parents the greatest degree of freedom, allowing them to begin the adoptive process whenever they are ready and to exercise control over what happens.

The easiest way to begin is to tell everyone you know that you are trying to adopt. This includes social workers, physicians, active church members in your community, school nurses or counselors, support groups for parents, nurse-midwives, high school principals, and therapists, as well as all of your friends.

Or you may decide to contact an adoption facilitator. This is an area in which the consumer must increasingly beware. Adoption facilitators are not agencies and may or may not be attorneys. They are not in any way licensed or regulated. They are consultants in a new field that is growing rapidly. For a fee, they will supply some or all of the following services: ideas for contacts or a list of contacts, training in writing a résumé to give to birth mothers, training in writing advertisements and compiling family photographs, and guidance in advertising and direct mailings to potential leads. They may do as little as bring the adoptive parents to the attention of a birth mother or they may do as much as take the adoptive parents through the full process and represent them in court.

While many adoptive parents locate children through independent or private means, the financial and emotional risks can be higher than when working with a reputable agency. If the adoptive parents have paid medical expenses or other expenses for the birth mother, and she changes her mind, they have no legal recourse to get their money back.

You have probably seen adoption advertisements everywhere. I have seen them on billboards and bus stop benches, not to mention the hundreds running in newspapers. They usually read something like this: "Loving couple wants to give your child a wonderful home." Although this approach is not for everyone, those who have diligently tried it say *it works!*

Couples who run advertisements and do direct mailings to adoption resources then install a special phone line or have their lawyer or facilitator screen the calls. In screening the calls, you will want to know the birth parents' ages, marital status, medical history, ethnic background, family situation, financial situation, and the due date for the baby.

Direct mailings consist of a photo-résumé and a cover letter detailing why the couple seeks adoption and giving information about their ability to raise a child. These letters are mailed to individuals or organizations who have contact with young people. The most effective way to do this type of campaign is to mail several copies of your photo-résumé to your friends and let your friends distribute them. A doctor who knows of a birth mother is more likely to be interested in your situation if it comes to his or her attention via a regular patient rather than a mass mailing.

One father who was willing to do this legwork comments:

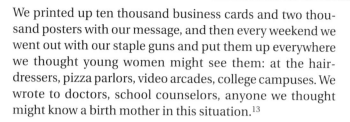

We printed up ten thousand business cards and two thousand posters with our message, and then every weekend we went out with our staple guns and put them up everywhere we thought young women might see them: at the hairdressers, pizza parlors, video arcades, college campuses. We wrote to doctors, school counselors, anyone we thought might know a birth mother in this situation.[13]

As a result of his efforts, he became the proud father of a baby boy.

Another family I know printed a folding business card with a photo of their family and a message to potential birth mothers expressing their desire to adopt again. It worked and they recently added a third child to their family.

The chart on the next page will help you compare the relative benefits of agency and independent adoptions.

How to Afford All This

When we were gathering resources for adoption expenses, we reasoned, "What better investment can we make?" We've always wanted to raise up a houseful of Christian children who would catch our passion for the Lord and maybe make a difference in the world.

The figures given in the chart for the possible cost of an adoption are only estimates. They do not include miscellaneous expenses, such as photocopies, long distance calls, document fees, attorney fees, or expenses related to immigration and naturalization.

Here are some ideas from Jerry Ann Jenista from her article "Financing an Adoption."[14]

1. Ask if your agency will allow you to make payments over time. The home study will take at least a few months. This could give you some time to assemble resources.

Agency	Independent
Range of Services Provided	
Most agencies offer complete services to both adoptive and birth parents.	Services may be limited to consultation and legal represen- tation or may extend to actually locating birth parents, depend- ing on the practitioner.
Costs	
May have a sliding scale. *Most* private agencies range from $10,000–20,000. Public agency fees are minimal to none.	Extremely varied depending on birth mother's medical and other expenses, attorney fees, and amounts spent on advertising, etc.
Adoptive Parents' Control over the Process	
Agency controls who may apply and how children are matched to families. Birth parents may choose adoptive parents. May have a long waiting period. Birth and adoptive parents may have varying degrees of contact or openness.	Adoptive parents have complete control over when to begin the adoptive process and how aggressively to pursue the process. Waiting period may be quite short. Legal and financial risks may be higher. Birth and adoptive parents may have varying degrees of contact or openness.
Custody and Guardianship of the Child	
On signing of consents, agency gets legal guardian- ship of child with temporary custody given to adoptive parents until adoption is finalized. Child *may* be placed in foster care until the period of time for revocation of birth parents' consent has expired.	Birth parents *may* place child directly with adoptive parents, instead of child going to foster care. Even though adoptive parents may have early custody of child, birth parents still have the right to revoke consent until period of revoca- tion has expired.

Agency versus Independent Adoption

Figure 2

2. Some agencies may allow you to swap services for some of their fee. For example, you could do office work or, if you are an artist, you might design a brochure for the agency.
3. Ask your church for help. Interested friends may hold a benefit or establish a fund for your family.
4. Do you have a relative or friend you can borrow money from?
5. Go to a finance company, credit union, or a bank.
6. Borrow money against your life insurance policy.
7. Get a home equity loan.

The expenses of an adoption and the cost of raising a child will probably cause some financial hardship. In our family, our adoptions have certainly had an impact on our lifestyle. There is usually insurance to cover biological pregnancies and births, but we had no insurance to cover the costs of our adoptions. As a result we live in a house that is inadequate for our needs. We must live very frugally and do without things that we might like to have. We have chosen to fill our home with children and love, rather than things. The family God has created for us is priceless.

Authors Wirth and Worden remind us of the lilies of the field: "They do not labor or spin. Yet I tell you that not even Solomon in all his splendor was dressed like one of these" (Matt. 6:28–29).

> Children can grow up much better in homes with abundant love and limited income than the contrary. Children in such families learn to share and save. They learn at a young age that spending money is earned not given, and they learn to look out for others. Those aren't bad lessons for young people to absorb.[15]

Your children won't remember the material aspects of childhood. They will remember the time you spent with them and the love you showered on them. These cost nothing and are far more important.

The National Adoption Foundation has a limited number of grants available for adoptive families. They also have located a few lenders who will loan money for adoptions at a competitive interest rate. (To inquire about either the grant program or loan sources, see appendix A for the address.)

The most affordable way to adopt is to study all the options and make a plan and stick with it. It is far more expensive to rush into something, discover it isn't the way you want to go, and then decide to start off in another direction.

EIGHT

The Home Study

once read, "If the unexamined life is not worth living, adoptive parents have the most worthwhile lives of all."[1]

There is something initially intimidating about the prospect of a home study. Your entire life and being will be under scrutiny. The event of a lifetime—potential parenthood—will be in the hands of one person, a stranger to you.

"Adoptive parents have to earn the right to parent," says Elizabeth Bartholet, a college professor and adoptive parent. "The notion that parenting is a privilege and not a right seems appropriate."[2] Undergoing the experience of a home study can make you feel less than privileged, making perspective important.

You can view the home study phase of adoption as an adversarial process or, as we did, an opportunity to learn more about yourselves, your opinions, and your family goals. We talked about things we hadn't talked about for a while (or ever) and learned some new things about each other. Few other life experiences offer such an opportunity for growth in a marriage. Rather than being intimidated or threatened by the home study phase, we immersed ourselves in it and benefited.

Wirth and Worden note, "You may think that you must be perfect to adopt a child, but you'll find very few super parents among adoptive parents—just people who cared enough to submit to scrutiny to find the child of their dreams."[3]

Orientation meetings held by many agencies are sometimes the place where potential parents can gracefully opt out of the adoption process. By the time you and your agency commit to a home study, the goal is not to screen you out but to make you aware of the challenges of adoptive parenting. In fact at this point, "There is a greater likelihood that a family will 'select out' than that a family will be turned down."[4]

What Is a Home Study?

Prior to considering a couple for adoption, an agency or sometimes an attorney will want to learn as much as possible about your marriage, your home, your goals and expectations of adoption, and your finances. At first blush this may seem to be an intrusive exercise. But consider the fact that these professionals are really investigating whether your child will have a safe, secure, happy environment in which to grow. "We look at a couple's strengths and weaknesses and their motivation to adopt," says Jennifer Hathaway, an adoption social worker with Bethany Christian Services. There is an intense focus on you and your marriage, but the more important focus is on the child. "We're really looking out for the best interest of the child," she says.

The home study is more contemporaneously known as the "adoptive family assessment," which really is a more accurate term and may sound less intimidating for some families. Its purpose is twofold, first, to ensure that your marriage and home environment are suitable for parenting a child and second, to help determine what type of child would be most appropriately placed with you. Underlying the process is the opportunity to prepare and educate the adoptive parents. During the course of our last adoption, our social worker was constantly sending us articles and things to read. She challenged us to think about the many issues involved in international adoption to prepare us. We felt confident to face the challenges of intercultural parenting because of her counsel.

When your file is accepted by an agency, you are usually assigned a social worker. You will have a number of meetings with him or her, with a minimum of one home visit. You will talk about a variety of things, but one meeting will usually focus on the husband and one will focus on the wife.

Some agencies may have group meetings where a number of applicants collectively discuss adoption issues. Whatever format is used, the home study will take several weeks to a few months, depending on the flexibility of everyone's schedule. It is usually valid for one year from the date of completion. If it takes longer than that to adopt, the study can be easily updated.

When you reach the completion of your home study, take the time to celebrate with your spouse! It is a milestone on your journey to becoming parents.

Papers, Papers, Papers

Prior to face-to-face home study meetings, most agencies will require you to submit a great deal of paperwork. Some documents may take time to locate or to order, so begin to think about assembling them even at this early stage so you will have them in your file.

We human beings lose papers. Make a few copies of documents that would be difficult or time-consuming to replace. If you are ordering certified documents, order a few copies. You may need them for immigration if you are adopting internationally or for a subsequent adoption.

The following is a list of documents and other information needed for most adoptions.

1. Birth certificate for each family member.
2. Marriage certificate and divorce decrees, if either partner has ever been divorced.
3. A physical exam form for each family member. Check to see how current these must be. Perhaps this is something you can schedule early on. If a statement of infertility is required by your agency, that will need to accompany your medical information.
4. Personal references. Anywhere from two to five will be required, depending on your agency. Some prefer non-relative references, and some require that at least one reference be a clergy person who is familiar with you and your family. Other references may be close friends, former teachers, coworkers, neighbors, or family friends. Be sure to notify these references that they will be contacted.

   The references may be asked to write a letter on your behalf, they may be interviewed over the phone, or they may be asked to come for a personal meeting. They should be prepared to discuss whether they believe you would be a good parent and whether they support your decision to adopt. If you don't currently have children, try to include someone who has seen how you interact with children and ask him or her to comment on that interaction in a letter. If you have a friend who is against the whole idea of adoption, it would probably be best not to use that person as a reference.
5. Employment verification.
6. Copies of bank statements, investment accounts, and other assets; plus verification of your indebtedness

(how much and to whom), including amounts you borrowed or intend to borrow for the adoption.

7. Income tax returns for the past two years.
8. Proof of medical insurance and a verification that your child will be covered when he arrives in your family.
9. Photos of you and any other children.
10. Fingerprints. Your agency may supply forms or they may direct you to your police station. Check their requirements.

Preparing for the Home Study

Make preparation for your home study a priority. More than likely, your eagerness will cause you to move mountains to meet your agency's requirements. Be accommodating to your social worker in terms of scheduling appointments. You will experience some inconvenience but accept it graciously. The child you may be getting is worth it.

Dress comfortably for your home study. If you want to dress up, do it, but if it is more your style to wear jeans and a nice shirt, wear those. Social worker Jennifer Hathaway notes, "You can't really prepare for a home study. You just need to be yourself." If that self wears jeans and usually has a coffee mug in hand, then don't go against what feels natural. Yet your heart must be prepared for adoption and your head must be ready to discuss some of the issues that will be raised during your study.

Most important, if your social worker seems uncomfortable about any aspect of your life story, be open and honest. If your childhood was not ideal, tell him or her what you gained from that experience in terms of how you will parent your own children. If you were arrested at age nineteen for marijuana possession or trespassing at an abortion clinic, tell your social worker. A thorough check of your criminal record will reveal your past. It will do more harm than good to be less than forthcoming.

If your past still haunts you significantly, perhaps you are not really ready for the adoption process. The best thing to offer your child is a reasonably "together" set of parents who are dealing successfully with their own past and present lives.

During your meetings, be natural. Most social workers can spot phoniness in an instant. "We're not looking for perfection," notes Jennifer Hathaway. "We just want honest answers. There really are no 'right' answers." You can freely discuss your reservations, fears, frustrations, and questions because they are all a natural part of the adoption process. Write out your questions in advance so you will get everything covered. In fact it would be a bit peculiar if you had no questions.

Bob and Maryann, a couple from Michigan, describe what to expect from a home study experience: "You'll be nervous, always wondering if you're answering their questions properly. You'll worry about how you will appear or come across to them as you sit face to face. You will have a lot of contact with your assigned social worker. You will always have questions regarding all the paperwork—from beginning to end."

They go on to say, "You'll worry about it all, and that's normal. It's all part of the adoption process and they will help and guide you all the way, as well as be supportive and help you get through this very anxious time." They conclude, "When you hold your child for the first time, you'll realize it was all worth it!" They have adopted two children from Korea, so they speak from experience.

Questions, Questions, Questions

You will be required to answer many, many questions, either verbally or in writing. Even if you are not required to write your answers to questions, it might be a helpful exercise to write your responses to the questions that appear in the rest of this section. It will give you a feel for how you will come across in your interviews and it will allow you to explore your motivations and thought processes.

Questions about You

- How would you describe yourself? What do you look like? How would you describe your personality?
- Do you have any hobbies?
- What was your childhood like? What are the ages of your siblings (if any)? Are your parents living?
- What are your happiest memories of your childhood? What are the unhappiest?
- Was religion a part of your upbringing? How do you feel about religion now?
- Describe your parents and their parenting. Did you like the way you were parented? What would you do differently?
- If they are living, are you close to your parents and siblings? How often do you get together?
- Is there a history of mental illness or alcoholism in your family?
- If you are infertile, how have you coped with this?
- How long have you been married?
- What are the strengths and weaknesses of your marriage?
- What interests do you share with your spouse?
- What do you like best and least about your spouse?
- How do you and your spouse resolve disagreements?
- If you were married previously, why was that marriage dissolved? How is your current marriage different?
- Why do you want to adopt?

You as a couple are already a family. Adopting a child is building on to your family. Your healthy marriage and love for one another are the building blocks on which you will structure your growing family. You will be welcoming this new child into a whole, intact system with whole persons as parents.

Questions about Your Parenting

- What are your dreams and hopes for your child?
- What do you think you will enjoy most about parenting?
- Are there any other adopted children in your immediate or extended family?
- What do you think will be difficult about parenting?
- What method will you use to discipline your child?
- How will you set rules in your family?
- If you have no children, what exposure have you had to children? (Baby-sitting, teaching Sunday school, day care, relatives, etc.)

Many people disapprove of spanking. Be sure you have researched this subject and agree with your spouse before committing to an answer to the discipline question. Your social worker will want to see that you have talked about it as a couple and come up with a game plan. The current popular methods are time-outs and withdrawals of privileges. If you need some more information before deciding on a method, there are several books at your library on theories of discipline.

It should also be noted that in some states, by state regulation, you are not allowed to use corporal punishment in a domestic adoption until the adoption is finalized. Make sure you are familiar with your state's regulations and are clear on the appropriateness of spanking before you commit to this as your method of discipline, particularly for very young children.

Questions about Your Home

- What will have to change about your current work, home, and recreational lifestyles to accommodate a child?

- Describe your house or apartment. What type of play space, both inside and out, is available? Will your child have a separate room?

You do not have to own a palace to adopt. Your house or apartment must be in reasonably good repair and large enough to accommodate another person. Most agencies do not require that the child have a separate room but will allow the child to share a room with a same-sex sibling.

"The most important thing is not material wealth," says Jennifer Hathaway. "It's the family's strengths." Keep this in mind if you have to delay some home improvements to pay for an adoption. You can always do the improvements later. No one will care if your carpet is worn as long as your heart is open and ready to love and accept a child. The agency will care that the environment is safe and that the child will have somewhere to play and parents to love him with all their hearts.

Do a safety inspection of your home. Have a smoke detector and a fire extinguisher on each floor and check that each is in good working order. Use common sense to make sure your house is free of hazards for a child. Although you do not have to have your home childproofed during the home study phase, it is a good idea to educate yourself about what needs to be done. There are a number of good books and videotapes at your library on how to do this. You may also inquire at your local hospital or fire department. By the time the home study is complete, most social workers will require that your childproofing be complete as well.

Questions about Child Care

- Will one spouse be available full-time to care for the child? For how long?
- If not, what arrangements can be made for child care, including during illness and emergencies?

- If you or your spouse will quit working outside the home when the child arrives, how do you plan to deal with the loss of income?

Some agencies will require one spouse to stay home full-time for a certain period of time. Try to ascertain what is expected and be prepared to do whatever it takes.

Questions about Siblings

- Do you have other children? List their names and ages.
- What are these children like, physically and emotionally?
- What have you done to prepare them for a new brother or sister?
- How do you think they will respond?
- If there will be racial or cultural differences, how have you prepared your children?

If you have other older children, they may be interviewed separately, as your social worker will want to know their feelings and attitudes about adopting a new family member.

Questions about Playmates

- Are there children of the same race or culture in your area as the child you are seeking to adopt? If not, how will you expose him to his race and culture?
- Do you have pets? How do they get along with children?

Be prepared to talk about what you will do to keep your child safe from your pet. And please, don't call your pet your "baby."

Questions about Adoption

- How do you feel about adopting?
- What worries you about adopting?

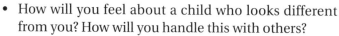

- How will you feel about a child who looks different from you? How will you handle this with others?
- How do you feel about your child's birth parents?
- What will you do if your child decides to search for his birth parents at some point?
- How will you talk to your child about adoption? What have you read or done to prepare yourselves for this?
- How does the rest of your immediate and extended family feel about adopting? Will they be able to welcome this new child?

Your Résumé

Some agencies may ask you to write a résumé type of document that may be shown to potential birth parents. It should contain all the basic information about your marriage and family, as well as some information about your personality, likes, and dislikes. Are you an outdoors person? Do you have extended family members nearby? What is the most important part of being a parent? You may also be asked to submit a good photograph of yourselves. Take great care in preparing these materials. Keep your focus on this: What would make a birth mother want to choose you? Like any of us, birth mothers have preferences, but accurately and positively highlighting your strengths as potential parents will be to your advantage.

Your Infertility

As mentioned previously, some agencies require demonstrated infertility before accepting you into their program and some do not. If you are required to demonstrate infertility, you will have to furnish medical evidence and you will also need to verify to your social worker that you have sufficiently resolved your infertility issues. Social workers will vary in their approach to infertility. Some will want to get the feeling that you have wholly put this issue to rest, and others will expect that the pain of infertility may linger. A social worker from Bethany Christian Services comments, "We want to see that you've released the issue and are ready to move on to adoption." In either case, "If you have gone through a soul-searching decision-making process, acknowledging your feelings of anger and pain, and if you have allowed yourself to grieve for the losses you have suffered and still wish to be parents more than you wish to be childless, you are probably ready to adopt."[5]

Another factor that an agency may consider is the length of time that has elapsed between ending infertility treatment and beginning the adoption process. Some agencies believe that a significant period of time should have gone by. There are two sides to this issue. If you are dealing with an agency that has a seven-year waiting list to adopt, it would be unreasonable to expect you to completely discontinue treatment during this time. On the other hand, it is understandable that an agency will be especially interested in this inquiry because infertility treatment is expensive, both financially and emotionally. Your social worker may want to be certain that you have the emotional and financial reserves to deal with the equally draining process of adoption.

The best policy here, as elsewhere, is honesty. Be open with your social worker about your journey from infertility to adoption. If you have received counseling or read specialized books, be prepared to discuss them. The best way to demonstrate to your agency that you are ready to adopt is to truly search your hearts and reach a place of peace and anticipation that reflects your readiness.

 ## NINE

The Waiting Game

Only in returning to me and waiting for me will you be
saved; in quietness and confidence is your strength.

Isaiah 30:15 LB

Adoption presents many opportunities to learn patience. First, there is the period of deciding to adopt. There is the wait for the home study. Next comes waiting for a referral. After the referral, you know there is a child, you may even have pictures to show, yet the child is not in your arms and you wait for an arrival date. Finally there is the wait for the actual arrival.

I am so blessed to have experienced both a biological pregnancy and an adoptive parent's waiting time. They each share some common characteristics: frustration, joy, fear, anticipation, and the need to rely totally on God's plan for our lives. So many people are affected by the wait. Your spouse, your other children, the rest of your family, and your friends will share in some of your emotions.

Twelve years ago Jan and John Markey from Michigan adopted a baby from Korea. They along with their three biological sons waited at home for her arrival. Jan says, "The last couple of months I remember having feelings of, Is our daughter ever going to arrive? One to two weeks before we knew she was coming home, I almost lost it. I remember crying on the phone to the head of the adoption agency and asking why, why, why are we waiting this long? I don't know to this day if this had any impact, but we soon got all the information on Katie's arrival schedule."

One adoptive parent comments, "Waiting to adopt puts parents in a peculiar kind of limbo. To guard against disappointment, we try to go about our lives as though nothing is going to change, but everything changes in an instant once a baby becomes available."[1]

When we received our referral for baby Grace, we were breathless with excitement. We had two photos of a living, breathing little human being who would be joining our family. One photo showed her peacefully sleeping. The other showed her squinting and crying her eyes out. We were frustrated that we couldn't see her eyes in either one. In each she was dressed in a ridiculously large white outfit and lying on a stark, white sheet. We made photocopies of the photos to send to relatives; we carried the photos everywhere and showed them to everyone; we gave our other children photocopies of her picture for them to decorate and make into welcoming cards.

Accepting the referral was a significant event. There was no turning back now. We couldn't change our minds. We figured that somehow Gracie was now counting on us. We told everyone she was coming but we didn't know when.

Wirth and Worden note, "Ironically, now that you are waiting for your child, it may be even harder. You may find yourself worrying about his health or wondering what she's doing. You may feel that every day of waiting is a day stolen from your life together."[2]

For us, the baby clothes came out of the garage to be washed. The crib was reassembled. The two bigger girls were happily sharing a room with a bunk bed. The other bedroom began to look like a baby's room. Gifts began to arrive. We were excited beyond belief.

The longer it took, the more frustrated we became. I can recall sitting in the rocking chair in her bedroom and crying, praying for patience for the rest of the wait for this child. In a biological pregnancy, the mother has the knowledge that the pregnancy will someday come to some conclusion. Waiting for an adoption holds no such assurances.

After the intensity of the home study and the excitement of choosing a country, a sense of letdown and even mild depression are not unusual. It may be hard to believe that the adoption will ever take place, especially if you've been told to expect a wait of six months or more. Some people feel that they are moving further away from adoption rather than coming closer to it.[3]

Bob and Maryann remind us, "You will have good and bad days. You can hardly stand the excitement some days, and others you'll be depressed, worrying that something isn't right, that it's taking too long, that your child is never going to arrive. But it will all work out."

Life is full of small joys and sorrows, milestones and detours. Adoption is no different. Through this experience, we can grow in wisdom, patience, and love. This waiting time is only the beginning of a lifetime of raising a child. Keep the long view, and the event will seem less frustrating. Our prayers were for Grace's health, safety, and nurturance while she was away from us. While you wait, you must trust that God is caring for and watching over this child until she arrives in your home.

What to Do While Waiting

Biological pregnancy is a time to prepare for parenthood. Adoptive couples require the same preparation. Use this waiting time to think about your expectations and hopes for yourselves and your child. Dare to dream! You will soon be "real" parents. Try to use this time to get ready for the challenge of parenthood. Adoption counselor Sharon Kaplan-Roszia says, "Adoptive parents are often robbed of pre-bonding experiences, but many of the ordinary things parents do to prepare themselves can be very helpful to adoptive parents, too."[4]

Keep busy while you're waiting. If you give yourself a list of assignments that must be completed, that will help you pass the time. You will feel great satisfaction as you tick items off your list. I distinctly recall conversations with my husband to this effect: "Wouldn't it be ironic if Korea closed its doors to adoption right as our turn was coming up?" I imagined the worst. Keeping busy helped keep my head on straight. Here are some suggestions.

Read everything you can about adoption. There are many fine Christian and secular books about adoption. The more prepared you are from reading, the more effective a parenting job you will do with your child. Arty Elgart says, "Reading about adoption is not only a way to gain information, it is also a good way to find some common ground when you need it, to connect with an author who understands."[5] Reading about someone else's story can make your feelings and reactions seem more normal.

Make arrangements for a leave of absence from work. The Family and Medical Leave Act (FMLA) guarantees adoptive parents a twelve-week leave if the employer has more than fifty employees. These leaves are usually unpaid, unlike a pregnancy leave. A biological pregnancy is covered by the federal Pregnancy Discrimination Act of 1978 and provides some financial compensation as a disability benefit for the biological mother. Most employers do not offer such equity to adoptive parents. Some enlightened companies offer a cash stipend to adoptive parents. This can be a few hundred to a few thousand dollars to help defray the cost of the adoption. If your employer offers such a benefit, count your blessings. Then don't forget to count it on your tax return as well. Such stipends are considered taxable income. As of this writing, a federal tax credit of up to five thousand dollars is also available to parents during the fiscal year in which their adoption is finalized.

Keep a journal of thoughts and prayers. Your child will be enchanted to someday learn of your emotional waiting time. Use it as a barometer of your ups and downs and to record some of the details of the waiting period. We take great delight in telling our children how we prayed for them while we waited for them to come to us. It teaches them the strength of our faith and demonstrates the faithfulness of our God.

Pamper yourself. Later you will long for moments of solitude. Go to the movies, get your hair done, indulge your hobby. If you don't have a regular exercise routine, start one. The stress reduction will help you tremendously. Long walks are good for the heart and are also good chances to dream and plan. Read those long novels you have been meaning to tackle. A six-hundred-page adventure story will seem tame compared to the adventure of parenting. Take a continuing education class on any subject that interests you. You may want to sew curtains or clothing for your coming child. Sewing is a great skill to have in financially lean, post-adoptive times.

Subscribe to adoption-related magazines. One of the best is *Adoptive Families*, available through Adoptive Families of America. If you can, send a subscription to the expectant grandparents. This will help to prepare and educate them on adoption-related issues.

Review your insurance policies. Chances are you have already contacted your health insurance carrier. Make sure that they have committed in writing to the addition to your family and that coverage will begin on placement, not on finalization. As you know, you may not get a final decree for many months, and you must have health insurance coverage for your child during this period.

If your employer offers group medical insurance as an employee benefit, there are some federal protections for adoptive parents. Under the Employee Retirement Income Security Act (ERISA) any group plan that provides coverage for dependent children of employees must provide the same coverage for adopted children. In addition, the coverage may not be restricted solely on the basis of any preexisting condition of the child at the time the child is placed. This law may be researched in detail at your local law library. The legal citation is 29 U.S.C. 1169.

If your company does not offer group medical insurance, it may have a self-insurance program. Most states have similar provisions in their laws providing for coverage of your adopted child under a self-insurance program just as any biological child would be covered.

When we adopted our first child, our carrier would not cover her until finalization, so we had to purchase some interim coverage. Sometimes this is called "gap coverage." It is extremely important to have this matter resolved before you hold your child for the first time because you will be responsible for her medical bills when she comes into your care.

What about life insurance? Do you need to change it or add your new child as a beneficiary? Do you want to check into a policy for your new child? One adoptive parent took out a policy on her son because the child had been adopted from abroad and they had used up all their savings. "We felt that if something were to happen to our child, we would not otherwise have the financial resources to undertake a second adoption," she noted. "We felt funny taking out the policy, but we did it."[6] We have whole-life insurance on each of our children. We also use it as a vehicle to build up a little savings for the college funds.

Plan for a will. While you may wait until the child's arrival to execute a will, begin to think about who would become the child's guardian in the event of a catastrophe or major illness. Be sure to explore how this guardian feels about adoption and raising an adopted child. What financial provisions can you make for child care in the event of the death of you or your spouse? While most of us don't like to dwell on these things, it is important to review these matters with your attorney now. You may be too busy to think much about your will after your child arrives. It seems so simple to draft a will. Many computer programs have "fill-in-the-blank" wills that are deceptively simple. When you actually confront all the issues in a will, it takes much longer than anticipated.

Organize photo albums. I made it a point to do this before the arrival of each child. I knew I would be too busy later, so I wanted to have them up to date before the new child's arrival.

Join a parents' support group. The best place to learn about parenting an adoptive child is through a support group with other adoptive parents. Support groups often offer cultural activities specifically designed for international-adoption families. (See appendix A to locate a support group.)

Make a friend. Have you met another couple who is going through the adoption process? Perhaps your social worker or adoption support group can help you find a buddy to help you through the waiting time. While that person will not serve the same function as a counselor or social worker, such friends will be the most understanding friends you have during this time.

Learn about your child's birth country and its customs. You may even want to contact a local college to ask if there are any students from that country attending classes. Inviting them to your home would be a welcome experience for them and would help educate you and your family.

Learn a little of the child's birth language. If you are adopting an older foreign child, although you will want to teach her English early on, a familiarity with her native language may help her feel more welcome. It may be the only way you can communicate in those first few weeks at home, other than the universal language of love, touch, and compassion.

Find out all you can about your child's previous care. Some children are carried in backpacks on the foster mother's back all day. If you knew this, this might be a way to soothe a cranky child. Some are accustomed to sleeping with an adult at night and may be afraid of a crib. I slept on the floor with my last daughter for several months almost every night holding her hand. It comforted her and felt natural for me to spend that time with her. A few trying nights I held her on my chest and let her feel skin-to-skin contact. It was good for both of us.

If your child is coming from an orphanage, she will have a major adjustment. She may be used to a tightly regulated schedule and may not have received much individual attention. She may be fearful and require extra doses of patience and understanding. If she has dealt primarily with women, she may be terrified of your husband. Time and lots of love can resolve most of these difficulties.

Read about or take a course on child care skills. Many hospitals offer such classes for expectant parents. For our first child, we made arrangements to view some videos at the hospital on changing diapers, bathing, and temperature taking. It would have felt a bit odd to go to a class with new biological parents, so I was grateful for the videos. Ask, ask, ask. Two nurses in Wisconsin, who are also adoptive parents, started a special program at their local hospital. Called "New Parents by Adoption," the four-session class covers topics such as feeding, bathing, illness, safety, and adoption issues. Many of the parents who meet in class continue to support one another after the arrival of their children.[7]

In many areas the group RESOLVE offers a Welcome Home Class. This is a parent preparation class for adoptive parents. Our local chapter's class has four weekly meetings covering such topics as baby basics, baby's health and safety, baby's needs and care, and bringing baby home. Contact the national RESOLVE office to find out if a class is offered in your area (see appendix A).

Take a CPR class. They are offered at many locations at a very low cost or even free. Call your local fire department, park district, or hospital for information.

Research nursing. I was so ill-prepared for my first child that I didn't even know this was possible. LaLeche League has a pamphlet on breastfeeding an adopted infant. It can also put you in touch with a local group leader or lactation consultant (see appendix A for the address and phone number).

Choose a doctor for your child and visit him or her even before your child arrives. We chose a pediatrician before our first child came, and she was of great help. She provided volumes of literature to read, and we knew she was there for us. We even called her at two in the morning in a complete panic over incessant crying. Would that have been possible had we not established our family with her first?

Give this doctor copies of any medical records you may have received. Discuss with him or her the type of tests or screening he or she would recommend after the child arrives. Make sure you know how your doctor feels about adoption. If he or she is less than enthusiastic about the idea, maybe you need to consult another doctor.

Find out from your social worker or attorney how much medical information you will have about your child. Ask for a family medical history if it has not been provided. Do you want to know about prenatal care and the course of labor and delivery? You may want to know if anesthetic was used or if labor was induced. Now is the time to inquire about these matters.

Make school arrangements if your child is older. If you are adopting a school-age child who has special needs, keep in mind that under United States Public Law 94-142 all handicapped children are entitled to free, appropriate public education. If your school system does not have facilities or teachers to meet your needs, it must make arrangements to have these services provided. If you think this may be an issue with your school, get started early on making arrangements and investigating various options.

Find baby-sitters or other child care. You can investigate centers and sitters well in advance of your child's arrival.

Design a birth announcement. This not only is fun, but also can help you focus and get through the waiting. When your child arrives and you have the specifics, you will be ready to take the announcement to the printers. We were even so compulsive as to address the envelopes before our babies arrived. It was an act of faith that we felt secure in doing.

Praying While Waiting

Proverbs 13:12 tells us, "Hope deferred makes the heart sick, but a longing fulfilled is a tree of life." I clung to this verse while waiting for our last child. I was certain that God would fulfill my longings or would teach me something I needed to learn if he didn't.

What if he hadn't? What if our adoptions had fallen through after all our plans and prayers? The next proverb reads, "He who scorns instruction will pay for it, but he who respects a command is rewarded" (Prov. 13:13).

All we can really pray for is that we are in God's will and that he will reveal that will in our lives. He doesn't make deals. We don't hand him a laundry list of requests and expect either immediate or long-term gratification.

In writing on fertility, author Jill Baughan suggests that we pray with an open heart and mind. "Everything we want may not be everything we need. What we are requesting may not be good for us right now. There's a fine line between asking God to fill our needs and dictating exactly how we want him to answer our prayers."[8]

God is not a vending machine who will fulfill our expectations and answer our prayers if we pray them correctly and approach him reverently, but he is faithful and merciful to give us what we need.

What about Your Partner?

Although you and your spouse are both committed to adoption, be prepared for periods when one or the other will express impatience, an inability to concentrate, or general crankiness. You may each take a different approach to waiting. One may be assertive, wanting to call the social worker twice a week. The other may be content to wait, which may be interpreted as a lack of caring by the assertive spouse.

When such feelings surface, remember they are normal. Try to share your feelings to the maximum extent possible. You may go through a phase where you feel like you're not ready to raise a child or that your relationship is insufficiently strong to withstand the stresses of a child. These doubts and insecurities are very common during the waiting period. You are dealing with a process over which you have no control. You are at the mercy of an adoption system. The more open and sensitive you stay to one another, the more you will be able to handle these down times.

Dr. James L. Moline warns couples:

> Watch out for the "cellophane wall," which is a deceptive barrier that begins to grow between two people experiencing extreme emotional challenges. Unlike the more obvious brick wall, this obstruction separates couples without their knowing it. Much like cellophane, this barricade is transparent but can still cause complete separation. You may be able to see your spouse, and even feel his or her hand through the membrane but everything will be obscured.[9]

I distinctly recall this phase while waiting for Grace. I felt like Mark was unemotional, detached, and too cool. He thought I was pestering our social worker by calling her too much. We didn't understand and appreciate each other's feelings. Men and women will process this time differently.

No matter how different we are, the important thing is for us to listen to one another.

Dr. Moline also suggests a weekly date night while waiting. Maybe you could attend a Marriage Encounter weekend or Family Life Marriage Conference (1-800-FL-TODAY). This is a wonderful opportunity to explore the strengths of your marriage at a time when it is healthy and expectant. Adoption counselor Arty Elgart suggests, "If the bad moments hit you as a couple, try taking a drive to the beach and walking together along the shore. That's the sort of thing that can have a calming effect on you when just about everything else fails."[10] Or better yet, take a vacation together. It may be a long time before you are able to be alone with your spouse. Seize the moment!

If things in your marriage have deteriorated significantly, you should consider professional assistance. Some indicators of this need are:

> You notice yourself unable to manage daily tasks that were once second nature. You no longer have the patience of Job. Your partner no longer has Job's patience either. You lose your temper in situations that formerly would not have bothered you. You are not as interested in working on your marriage. You lose interest in sex. Your appetite changes. You have difficulty sleeping. You feel down in the dumps, sad, depressed. You are excessively hard on yourself about things you have little to no control over.[11]

Early intervention with such feelings can make them more bearable and short-lived and is a good investment in making you a healthier marriage partner and parent for your child.

The Rest of the Family

Discuss the adoption and share your excitement with family and friends. Remember they may need to be educated about adoption and may not be totally sensitive or supportive. Some adoptive parents have heard, "How can you raise someone else's cast-off child?" You may receive some strong reactions, but with your patience and excitement, and a little bit of training, your family will soon share your enthusiasm. There is nothing like a child to bring stubborn adults together. You and your family will soon become walking ambassadors for adoption.

While you deserve sensitivity, Patricia Irwin Johnston reminds us that there are certain things your family should be able to expect from you. Among them are:

> Information. "People can't be sensitive about something they don't understand."
>
> Sensitivity. Your decision to adopt may cause pain for others, such as grandparents who are mourning the loss of a grandchild who will share their genetic heritage.
>
> Patience. Your family may need time to adjust to your decisions, especially controversial ones, such as an international or interracial adoption.
>
> Openness. If people say hurtful things, they must be made aware of the inappropriateness of their comments. Privately educate them and tell them your concerns.
>
> Clarity. Keep the information you pass along simple. Most people aren't going to be interested in the minute details or the emotional heaviness of your experience.
>
> Honesty. "Openly discuss your concerns and your hurt feelings with relatives who are unwilling to consider your child one of the family. If they still won't budge in their attitudes, don't continue to beat yourself up by trying to educate them over and over again. For your child's sake, the best method for coping with these few is by avoiding them."[12]

On a practical level, take a friend or relative along with you when you shop for the new arrival. Ask friends and relatives to keep their eyes open at garage sales for baby needs. Just as preparing for any other child, the more hands-on the experience, the more others are able to share the excitement.

Choosing a Name

One of the most significant ways to involve your family is in the choosing of a name. When we were waiting for Grace, we sat around at my brother's house on several occasions and went over names. The aunts, uncles, cousins, and nieces all contributed. Choose one that will honor a family member. If you are adopting internationally, choose one that preserves a cultural identity as well.

Wirth and Worden write, "Most Americans give their foreign-adopted children American first names to aid in their adjustment. Many keep a native middle name (possibly the child's birth name)."[13] With our last child, we had chosen the name Grace long ago, but kept her Korean first name preserved as her middle name.

Experts advise that you keep at least part of the child's birth name, regardless of the age of the child, to strengthen the feeling of acceptance of the child's past. This is especially important with international adoptions. However, children adopted from abroad may have names that are unfamiliar to us.

To help your child have an easier time in school, you may want to give him or her a new, American sounding first name while keeping part of your child's given name as the middle name. However, a child adopted at an older age from another country may prefer to keep his or her original first and middle names even if they are difficult for friends and teachers to pronounce.[14]

Author Deborah McCurdy says:

Choosing a first name or a middle name from your child's country affirms your child's cultural and national heritage as an important part of him. It demonstrates to your child and to the world that his original culture is a source of pride. It is an open acknowledgment of a positive kind of difference that will always be part of your child. It may be especially important as your child grows older, but having a typical American name as well may be just as important. Your child can then have the best of both his worlds. A birth country name combined with an American name gives the child the opportunity to affirm either side of his or her cultural identity, depending on the child's mood and stage of development.

She goes on to note that a child named John Carlos Clark could call himself John C. Clark or J. Carlos Clark depending on his preference at different ages.[15]

Siblings

Other children can be involved and excited with you. Talk about what it will be like with the new addition. Read books about adoption and about new siblings. Several good books are listed in appendix D. Adoptive mother Jill Bull says she had her older child pray with the family for whatever stage they were in their adoption. The child remained informed and felt like a part of the process. Check with your local hospital about new sibling classes and decide if this will be appropriate. If you are adopting an infant, your older child could learn a great deal at a sibling class, as such classes touch on issues of adjustment and jealousy. Also, to the extent that a child is able to care for a baby, they learn about infant care.

Preparing Your Home

Decorate the room, if you feel so inclined. If the adoption falls through, however, it will be painful to look at the room. But if your child does indeed arrive, you will have your home prepared. Adoptive parent Terra Trevor said of her second adoption,

> I let myself do the nesting and preparing I had been afraid to do the first time. I purchased a few special toys and made a flannel patchwork quilt. This time I knew that even though I'd be heartsick if the adoption didn't go through, there was no way to save myself from the hurt. I figured I might as well have fun with the planning. I told myself I could give the things I had gathered to charity if need be. Thus, I gave myself permission to be excited. It was a positive effort that would lead to good one way or the other.[16]

We decided that if our last adoption fell through, we would give all the baby items to the local crisis pregnancy center so we could help support a mother who had chosen to parent her child.

Childproof your home, depending on the age of your child. At minimum, inspect your smoke detectors to make sure they are in working order. If you are adopting a toddler or walking child, you will want to secure cabinets, make sure rugs don't slide, and have a gate or two to secure off-limit areas of your home.

Prepare the child's storybook. Some families make a scrapbook of all the materials related to their adoption. Others prepare an introductory book or family storybook. Author Angela Elwell Hunt suggests:

> If you are adopting an older child, you might make a book that will introduce your family. Into a photograph album or scrapbook, insert pictures of your home, family pets, you and your spouse, the family car, the grandparents, etc. You might tell the family story and begin with a wedding picture. Under each photo, write part of your story beginning with, "Once upon a time, Jim and Janet fell in love and were married." Under a photograph of the family home, write, "A little while passed and Jim and Janet wanted to share their home with a

child, so they prayed and asked God to send them a very special child."[17]

Years and years will pass, and your child will still be excited when you announce, "That very special child was *you!*"

Save some chores until the end. Assign the last day to sterilizing bottles and stocking up on formula and baby food. It will help the day of arrival pass more quickly. My ploy was to carry a can of formula, an opener, and bottles to the airport. When the arrival of our flight was announced, the older girls and I got busy filling bottles because we figured the baby would be hungry. It made that last waiting time at the airport easier and was a productive use of nervous energy.

Don't view waiting time as wasted time. Treasure each day of your life. Don't wish away the wait, for you will squander a season and look back to wonder where these precious moments went.

 TEN

Your Child Arrives

Life is a blend of joy and pain; so is the adoption
experience.

Angela Elwell Hunt

At long last you are notified that your child is ready to
come home. Ready or not, you are about to become
parents.

If you go to an airport to meet your child, bring a
few items of clothing, especially travel clothes appropriate for the weather, a blanket, and a few toys. Your social
worker may have other suggestions as to what will be needed
that day, depending on your child. If you will be traveling
home any distance, be sure to bring some formula for the
young child. A cooler to keep it fresh can make a long drive
home more enjoyable for everyone. We have a plastic cooler
with a refreezable ice block for carrying bottles. It is small
but holds six bottles along with the ice block. It has accom-
panied each of our children on many journeys.

Even if you have read every book about adoption and raising children, you will probably still feel somewhat insecure.
Lois Gilman comments, "The parents of newborns can fol-

low some basic advice: If the baby's wet, change him; if he's hungry, feed him. Parents who adopt non-newborns may grope around for other answers."[1]

If you are feeling depressed or overwhelmed, be assured these feelings are normal. Your whole life has just turned upside down. Your family is changing. Your relationship with your husband will change. You may feel totally incompetent to deal with this new chapter in your life.

As important as the support of other parents was in the waiting phase, it is perhaps even more important now. Be sure to maintain those contacts you have made with adoptive support groups. They may serve as an invaluable source of advice and comfort for you.

Make time for yourselves as a couple. You will feel guilty for doing so, but you shouldn't. The best parents are those who don't neglect their own needs. They recognize the primacy of the marital relationship and take the time and make the effort to strengthen that bond.

If your company offers a parental leave, take it. Otherwise, try to make some other type of arrangement so everyone can be home together initially. Even if dad has to use up vacation time, this will be time well spent as your whole family adjusts to this new development.

The First Few Weeks

Even the youngest children will grieve to some extent because of the dislocation they have experienced. Your child may seem offish and nonresponsive to your efforts at comfort. He may even seem angry and stiffen up as you try to cuddle him. The main thing your new child needs is assurance that you will meet his needs promptly and lovingly. From that he can build the basis of a trusting relationship.

When you find something that comforts your child, repeat it. Tune into his prior routine as much as possible. This is where the information you obtained from your social worker about the child's likes, dislikes, and lifestyle will come into play. Meet his needs as promptly as possible, and over time the child will discover that he can depend on you and that you belong together.

If your child is arriving from overseas, he will be exhausted from the flight and will have his days and nights mixed up. It will take him at least a week to become readjusted.

When our daughter Grace arrived, I actually slept with her on the floor and held her hand for the first few months almost every night. The result was a child who was very secure but who didn't sleep through the night until we bit the bullet when she was fourteen months of age and let her cry it out.

Intellectually I had always known that crying never destroyed a child and at this point I was certain the lack of sleep would destroy us. After a few days of firmness, she finally assumed a normal sleeping schedule. Some sleepless months could have been avoided had we been firm earlier.

Yet I wouldn't have traded our bonding time sleeping on the floor together for a year of good sleep. When she would wake up, sometimes all she wanted was to hold my hand to know that someone was there. I'd clutch her chubby hand and gently stroke her head, and she would go back to sleep.

When our first daughter arrived at three days old, she was small enough to fit into a cradle. Grandpa had handcrafted an oak family heirloom that we kept next to our bed. Every twenty minutes or so, I would check on Clare in her cradle. "Is she breathing okay?" my husband would ask. Sometimes I would wake up to find Mark just staring at her sweet, sleeping face.

There is something magical about nighttime with a new child. The house is still and you have quiet, uninterrupted time to savor a new life—to learn your child's sounds, feel his touch, and enjoy his smell.

Your Adjustment as Parents

The announcement of pregnancy is usually received joy-ously. The announcement of an adoption is not always met with such excitement. Some adoptive parents may even have to explain or justify their actions. Lois Gilman writes, "Lacking also are traditional rituals, such as baby showers, to celebrate the impending arrival. Familiar steps of validation and attachment that families follow before a child's arrival are thus absent or short-circuited in adoptive families."[2]

We were fortunate to have friends who hosted a baby shower for each of our children, no matter how they arrived. Friends, family, and colleagues shared with us the excitement and anticipation of the expected child. They also let us feel their love and support.

Adoptive parents are notoriously hard on themselves. We expect to be perfect parents. We think everyone else expects us to be perfect because, well, we *chose* parenthood. We've had to prove ourselves "worthy" to become parents by passing a home study and other scrutiny. Now that we are real parents, we feel that we will somehow be immune to frustration, anger, or rejection, which are feelings common to all parents. Because of this presumed expectation, we are reluctant to express some of the normal frustrations of parenting.

Stephanie Siegel notes, "New parents are usually overly conscientious and intense about raising their first child. Through inexperience and feelings left over from childhood, they may develop rigid standards for themselves. They are well aware of the mistakes of their parents and have no desire to repeat them." She adds: "The notion of being a perfect parent is only a fantasy."[3]

Attachment

In the early difficult days with a new child you may question the wisdom of your decision. The doubts and insecurities are normal. Many a parent has come to the experience of parenthood with a shocking jolt. They have looked at their red-faced, squalling new infant and wondered if they could ever love this creature. They have faced the reality of parenting and have had to give up the fantasy of the perfect child, and the perfect parent as well.

I often wondered if holding my new children would make me feel an instant bond with them. It didn't. Although I was delirious with excitement each time I held a new child, the feelings had to grow to authenticity through the simple rhythms of building a life together.

Holly van Gulden and Lisa Bartels-Rabb write:

> After the initial excitement of having a new child wears off, parents sometimes become concerned if they do not "feel" love for the child. . . . Parents who have given birth to their children experience these same emotions. In fact, it is normal for the primary caretaker (usually the mother) to take from two to six months to form strong love feelings for her child, and it can take even longer for the other parent. It simply takes time for the initial infatuation parents feel for their children to grow into a deeper love. And once the realities of parenting hit and the infatuation subsides, you may feel a bit ambiguous while your love for your child is under construction.[4]

You need to take it easy on yourself and not expect instant love and devotion. Through the simple process of living together and caring for your child, your feelings will grow and blossom.

This is the time for you to become attached and to fall in love with your child. An infant will grow attached as you consistently meet his needs in a positive manner. He will learn that you are a safe person and that you can be trusted. Remember, "attachment occurs over time and involves consistent activity on the part of the parent to meet the physical and emotional needs of the child."[5]

Psychologists are debating the whole theory of bonding. The theory was that a child needed to bond with his mother immediately after birth and if he didn't, he would have difficulty bonding with anyone in life. If you missed this early time frame to bond with your child, you had blown it.

More enlightened theorists distinguish between bonding and attachment. A child may bond with an early caregiver, but that does not mean he cannot become attached to a subsequent caregiver, such as an adoptive parent. Attachment is a closeness that grows over time. The adopted child can become attached to a new parent, even if the child previously had spent time with a different caregiver. "Once a child has bonded with one caregiver, such as a birth parent or a foster parent, the bond can be transferred to another caregiver: an adoptive parent."[6]

Psychologists who have studied children and adoption conclude that there is little difference in the quality of attachment between adopted and non-adopted infants and their parents. In fact in this respect, "adopted mother-infant pairs tend to look almost exactly like biological pairs. Differences don't show up until infants are past the age of six months."[7]

Although the subject of attachment disorders is beyond the scope of this book, you should know that adopting a child over six months in no way dooms that child to a life of feeling unattached to his parents. There are many things that adoptive parents can do to encourage this bond. Jayne Schooler says:

> Parents can best rebuild the shattered heart of the withdrawn child by developing consistent ways to express love. Positive, constant reinforcement of the child's sense of value and worth, with assurance that the child's worth is not based on performance, will eventually fill the empty places.[8]

The importance of the attachment process cannot be underestimated. It helps children feel safe and loved. It affects their socialization, intellectual development, and identity formation. The more attention you are able to devote to the attachment process, the greater the benefit to you and your child.

Stages of Bonding

Dorothy Smith and Laurie Nehls Sherwen are two nurses who have studied mothers and adopted children and the bonding, or attachment, process. They have identified three stages of bonding in adoption.[9]

The first time frame consists of bonding activities prior to adoption.

1. Mother attains role identity
2. Mother fantasizes about infant/child-to-be
3. Mother problem-solves through fantasy
4. Mother problem-solves through manipulating environment
5. Mother develops a support group
6. Mother carries out nesting behaviors (prepares infant's/child's clothes, room, etc.)

The second time frame identifies bonding activities at the time of adoption, or entry of the child into the home.

1. Mother is active participant and maintains control
2. Mother has opportunity for immediate and prolonged contact with infant/child
3. Significant others are present
4. Significant others acknowledge/give attention to infant/child
5. Significant others acknowledge/give attention to mother
6. Mother begins to nurture
7. Father interacts and begins to nurture infant/child
8. Attendant professionals give support

In this second time frame, we see the participation of other family members. These significant others, such as extended family members, are an important part of this process. The greater the support and acceptance of all family members, the better the bonding experience between the parents and child.

The third time frame identifies the bonding activities that occur after adoption.

A. Mother
   1. Touches and explores infant/child
   2. Engages in non-verbal communication
   3. Engages in verbal communication (high-pitched tone for infant)
   4. Allows body contact with infant/child
   5. Interacts in rhythmic patterns with infant
   6. "Identifies" infant/child
   7. Feeds, bathes, clothes infant/child
B. Infant/Child
   1. Engages in non-verbal or verbal communication with mother
   2. Responds to maternal nurturing behaviors
   3. Elicits physiological response in mother
   4. Meets mother's rhythms

Who hasn't observed the automatic sway that women acquire when standing while holding a child? Have you noticed that voices go up a few octaves when talking to a baby? These are all common, predictable, observable stages of the bonding process. It may be comforting to know that the nesting behavior and cooing you have been experiencing are all part of God's wonderful plan for us to nurture our babies, however they come to us.

Agency Follow-Up

Most adoption agencies will require post-adoptive sessions, at least one of which will be in your home. You may resent this continuing intrusion, but keep in mind that the agency is looking out for the child. The court that will complete your adoption also wants to know that the placement is working. There may also be others, such as birth mothers or connections in the child's country of origin, who will want a status report on the child.

There may be as many as five visits to your home. These people really want to know how you are doing and they may have valuable advice for you if you are having difficulty.

They want to know if the baby is having physical problems and if you are adjusting to parenthood. They want to know how the other members of the family are faring. How are other children adjusting? How are the logistics of work, trips, church, and baby-sitters working out? If you have doubts or questions, *now is the time to bring them out.* Sometimes a listening ear or some short-term counseling can redeem a difficult situation.

Celebrate!

Following this post-placement study you will be ready for court finalization of your adoption. You will have jumped through your final hoop. After navigating this sometimes complicated maze, finalization is a deeply satisfying event.

This is the time to express your family's uniqueness and creativity. You can design any kind of celebration you want. You can keep your joy private, but we chose to have a little ceremony in our home.

Because our backgrounds are a blend of Catholicism and Protestantism, we had a blended "baptism" ceremony for Grace. We wrote out a ceremony in which we promised to raise our child in the Christian faith. The older children handed the baby a stuffed lamb to welcome her into our family. We lit candles, one for each family member, and a family garment was placed on the baby to symbolize her adoption into our family.

Prior to her arrival we sent out squares of muslin to friends and relatives and asked them to decorate them in a fashion that would represent them or their families. Some people embroidered elaborate messages; others used simple fabric paint to express their feelings. My mother-in-law sewed and quilted the pieces together for a special wall-hanging for Grace's room. It is a constant reminder of the joy that surrounded her arrival.

Another idea is to ask friends and relatives to bring a perennial to plant in your garden. Each year when the plant blooms, you will have a living reminder of this milestone in your lives.

During the early days at home it is probably a good idea to limit guests. Your child must learn who you are and you must learn who he is. A child can become overwhelmed with too much excitement. You will have a lifetime together to remember this event.

Anniversaries

Some parents choose to have anniversary celebrations to mark their child's arrival date. These can be private, family affairs, or you might choose to have a party. Some families call this "Gotcha Day."

Celebrations or rituals take on an enhanced importance in the adoptive family. They provide a way to promote belonging in your family. For an adopted child, this is a major task.

Light a candle. Adoptive mother Jill Bull says she will celebrate her daughter's adoption with a candle ceremony of four candles: one for God, one for the birth mother, one for the adopted child, and one for the adoptive family as a whole.

Write a letter. If your child is older and is struggling with some adoption issues, have him write a letter to his birth mother on this day. It doesn't have to be sent off anywhere, but in it your child can express his feelings and confront some unresolved issues.

Donate a book. You may want to donate a book about adoption to your child's school on the anniversary date each year. School libraries may not have much information about adoption. They would welcome the addition.

Send announcements. Some families send announcements of the anniversary and ask people to send a contribution to their agency in lieu of a gift to the child. This can help some other family share the joy of the adoptive experience.

Write a play or song. One family wrote out a play detailing how each child came to the family. Mom and Dad improvised a stage and served popcorn to the kids. The kids sat completely mesmerized while the parents lovingly told the story of their family's beginnings. It was not elaborate or fancy. It was just profound and meaningful.

If your children are older, *they* may be interested in writing out the story of your family and how it came together. Maybe a musically inclined child can write a family song for everyone to learn and sing together.

Celebrate the siblings. You may want to celebrate brother/ sister day. If you have more than one child, the children give each other a gift and thereby celebrate their relationship.

Add to the life storybook. Use the anniversary to add pages to your memory or life book. You may want to include a current photo of the child on this date along with some current interests and accomplishments.

Make a poster. Some families make a poster with the child's arrival photo in the center. Each year on anniversary day they add a photo to show how the child has grown. This creates a continuous record of your lives together.

To celebrate birthdays, make a birthday poster for your child. Put his current photo in the center and list all the ways that he is special. Emphasize *who he is*, not *what he does well*. This can help your child appreciate his uniqueness. It gives you the opportunity to express your admiration simply for who your child is. As a part of this poster, use your child's name, with each initial used to name a special quality. (Example: CLARE—Creative, Loving, Always-helpful, Reader, Enthusiastic.)

Visit a museum. If you have adopted internationally and your child is old enough, visit a museum or embassy of your child's birth country.

Buy a book. Buy a new adoption book for your child. There are books available for every age group (see appendix D). Each year you can add to your child's library with an age-appropriate book to help you keep the dialogue open in your ongoing adoption discussions.

Treasure these things in your heart. Adoptive mother Pam Walsh says that they really only celebrate their child's birth date, but there are many days that she celebrates privately in her heart, such as the first time she held her daughter, the day she brought her home, the first court date, the second court date, and the date the papers were signed.

Make it a family affair. Lois Melina celebrates adoption day as a family celebration rather than an individual celebration.

> Rather than receiving presents, the child whose homecoming day we are observing, gets to select an activity that the entire family can participate in, such as going out to dinner, going to a movie, or going for a swim. The emphasis is on our family celebrating the child's arrival, rather than on the child celebrating joining a family.[10]

In our family, most days are a celebration. When a day marks an event in our lives together, it always takes on some special quality—whether public or private, large or small.

ELEVEN

Talking about Adoption

Experts agree that there is no magical time to begin to talk about adoption. Carolyn Chamberlin, a counselor with Marywood Maternity and Adoption Services of Austin, Texas, is quoted in an article in *Children Today.* She believes that adoption is a

life-long experience that should be an ongoing cycle of understanding throughout an adoptee's life. Chamberlin believes there should never be a time in a child's life when she is unaware of her adoption, even when she is too young to discern what it means. According to Chamberlin, adoption should be a concept the child grows to understand as she matures.[1]

Treat adoption as a natural part of your family life. When your child finally arrives, there is a tendency to want to just relax and act like any other family. You can certainly be a normal family but you have ahead of you a lifetime of dealing with adoption issues. The more prepared you are for them, the better will be your adjustment as an adoptive family.

We tell our children they all came from God and are God's children. They each came to us in different ways and became a part of our family. We don't make a big deal out of adoption, but we don't deny it either. We just acknowledge it as a part of our family life. We may have come together through adoption, but it is love that binds us together as a family.

Each child has a life story. That story starts with how the child came to her family. For a biological child, it starts with the day she was born. For an adopted child, it starts with the day she entered the family.

The day of birth and day of arrival are usually photographed excessively. Put those photos in a book. Some parents call this a "life book" in which they chronicle the arrival of any new member of the family. The book contains photos and other mementos. Share the joy and excitement with the children. If you treat adoption this way, the children will gradually, naturally begin to ask questions. Be prepared to simply and honestly answer them. Keep the focus on your love and commitment to the child. How, where, and when she arrived is incidental by comparison.

Sometimes truths can be discussed more freely in the context of a book or a story. The books listed in appendix D deal with several different aspects of adoption and are some of the best available to use to begin or encourage the dialogue with your child.

In the earlier days of adoption, when agencies made a point of matching children with adoptive parents of similar physical characteristics, some parents never told their children they were adopted. This could come as quite a shock later in life when the adopted child learned of his true origins.

Our families are different now. There are many variations on the family theme. Your adopted child is likely to know other adopted children as well as children who are part of stepfamilies or who live with a single parent. "What this means is that the adopted child no longer must worry that his home situation is different from those of his classmates. Everyone's situation is unique and no one should be ostracized because of that."[2]

Acknowledge that your family may be different but emphasize your love and commitment to one another. Rather than ignoring differences or denying the truth of adoption, such an openness holds five advantages for your child, according to adoption expert Jayne Schooler.

> First, it builds a trusting relationship between parent and child. . . . Second, this open style integrates missing pieces from the child's past. . . . Third, open disclosure corrects erroneous views of the past as, fourth, it helps the child sort out realities and fantasies. . . . Fifth, this straightforward approach helps form a foundation for identity information.[3]

How would you rather have your child learn of her adoption? By a crude remark from a relative who lets out a family secret? Or by you and your spouse conveying the information in a consistent, loving, accepting fashion?

Talking with Your Child

The more comfortable you are with the idea of adoption, the more that comfort will be conveyed to your child. The tale of your child's adoption is not a fairy tale—it is your child's life story, and the way you treat that special story reveals your own feelings about adoption, which are then transmitted to your child.

Sometimes there can be too great an emphasis placed on an adopted child's being special. This emphasis can create enormous pressure on children to *be* special, rather than just to be themselves. A fourteen-year-old adoptee, quoted by Laura Giardina, says, "I'm not special, I'm just me."[4] There is no danger, however, in always reassuring your child that she is special to *you*. Some well-meaning relatives may continuously refer to your child as special because of the fact of the child's adoption. Although this is an innocent mistake, talk it over with the relative before it becomes a problem.

Sometimes parents overemphasize the fact of their child's adoption, and it is not good to err on that side either. Lois Melina says:

> Sometimes, in a well-meant effort to accustom a child to thinking of himself as adopted so he "always knows," a parent may say, "Where's my adopted little girl?" or "What a handsome little adopted boy!" But while it is natural to say to your child, "What a handsome little boy!" it isn't natural to say, "What a handsome little adopted boy!" By hearing about adoption in such artificial contexts, even young children can pick up the idea that adoption is something that makes them different from other children, when it is the way they joined their families that is different.[5]

Strom and Donnelly write that overemphasizing adoption

> can be just as bad as ignoring it. If you are always talking about your children's adoption, you will be emphasizing that they are different. This is certain to make them uncomfortable. The key is to strike a balance. Don't remind them too much, but mention it often enough to be sure that the idea is accepted and natural.[6]

Very Young Children

Studies reveal that parents who have resolved all issues—including infertility and parenting another person's biological child—are far more likely to raise children who are comfortable with adoption. Both children and parents experience losses in adoption and, for the parents, these must be worked through in these early years.[7]

A very young child will sense how a parent feels when the parent uses the word *adoption* and other adoption language. If the child senses the parent's ease with talking about adoption, she will be at ease as she develops and the words begin to have some meaning for her.

Preschoolers

Children ages four, five, and six generally accept being adopted. They live in the here and now because they cannot compare their life to any other. "They don't understand yet that most children live with their biological mother and father, but even if they did, they would be unlikely to care that their family is different."[8]

A child can't understand adoption until she understands how people are made. Then she can grasp that some babies don't stay in their family of origin. "Some psychologists maintain that, until a child is old enough to understand sex, he is not old enough to understand adoption."[9]

Children will usually bring it up—"Did I come from your tummy?" This is the time to start filling in details of how they came to be adopted. Use age-appropriate language to tell them what they need to know when they need to know it. Don't force them to try to understand something they are not prepared to grasp.

Your child must know that she was born, just like every other child. Some adopted children may conclude that they were never born because of the constant emphasis on how their family was formed. They may even feel like some kind of alien who came to the world like no other being. It is important to know that the adoption story starts with a birth.

At about this time, children will begin to notice differences in skin color or other physical characteristics. They must know that you are comfortable with your family and that you focus on your ties and love. They must know that it is okay to wonder about all of this and to be able to talk to you about it. Support them in their quest for information.

What if your child never asks questions about adoption? If it hasn't come up in any meaningful way by age four or five, you should initiate the discussion, perhaps by reading an age-appropriate adoption book.

School-age Children—Ages 7–11

Children ages seven to eleven are influenced by their peers and schoolmates. They gain a greater awareness of the world because of their exposure to it. They learn that people are different, because they meet different people. Perhaps most important, they realize that most people in the world are *not* adopted. This makes them want to know why they are not like everyone else and what they have lost from their family of origin by being adopted. It is at this age that they begin to wonder what their birth parents were like and why they placed them for adoption. They may also begin to experience sadness and anger as they grieve over the life that might have been.

We all want our children to be mentally healthy. One way to promote this health is to model an attitude that says, Life may be hard sometimes, but it can be dealt with. A child who feels she can deal with some of the uncertainties and unknowns in life will manage quite well.

When the child's testing behavior erupts, as it inevitably will, you can honestly approach it with the attitude that this is your kid and that you will love her no matter what. If you have demonstrated to your child that difficulties and uncertainties in life can be dealt with, you and your child will be able to go successfully through some of the difficult stages of growth.

At ages seven to eleven, children begin to understand that they have had a significant loss in their lives—the loss of birth parents. This realization may cause your child to go through intense insecurity and grief. It is important to allow your child to express these feelings. The child needs the security from you to explore and process conflicting emotions. Encourage her to write about her feelings or attend an adoption group. If needed, let her talk things over with a counselor. Children can also use art, music, poetry, or physical activity to help work through their feelings.

Children may begin to think that there was something wrong with them that caused their birth parents to "give them up." Let your child fully explore and discuss her feelings, however irrational they may be. Illustrate in whatever way you can that there was nothing wrong with her. Perhaps she can see medical records or social worker reports that documented her as a happy, healthy child before she came to you, certainly not one who was defective and unlovable.

Focus on the birth mother's circumstances. "Whatever the circumstances, emphasize that it was her circumstances and not some quality in the child or lack of concern for the child that resulted in the adoption plan. Placing a baby for adoption is done by a woman who at this point in her life feels unable to care for a child."[10] With this emphasis, your child will know that her adoption was not her "fault" because she was "defective."

Middle Childhood

At middle childhood children are coming to a better sense of themselves as distinct individuals. Often this distinctness comes as the result of comparison: How do other families look, how do they live, how much money do they have? "Children this age grapple to understand what differences mean outside the family."[11]

They may ask difficult questions. Lois Melina suggests, "Let the child take the lead. If she is asking a question, she probably is prepared to deal with the answer. In fact, she may be more able to deal with the answer than the parent."[12]

The best thing for adopted kids is to be exposed to other adopted kids. This is another benefit of a support group. Through that group your child can meet and talk with other adopted children. Between your discussions with your child and her discussions with other adopted children, she can acquire the tools to deal with the attitudes of others, as well as cope more effectively with her own feelings.

Continue to portray your child's adoption as something positive. It is the way you built your family. Focus on the fact that there wasn't anything wrong with her, but rather her birth mother was trying to provide as well as she could for her child.

Always try to portray birth parents in a positive light. Stress that the birth mother made an adoption plan because she loved her child, not because she merely wanted to be rid of her.

It is common for school-age children to fantasize about their birth parents. On a bad day, they will fantasize about how great they must be, compared to you! Don't feel threatened. It is a normal part of attempting to piece together an identity.

One adoption expert suggests keeping up a life book for your child. Although these books have traditionally been used to prepare older children for a move to a new family, they can be an important way to preserve a childhood for any child in the family. Their purpose is to be a chronicle of the child's life prior to entering the adoptive family. For an infant, that story will be quite short; for an older child, it may be substantial.

The book chronicles key events—birth, foster care, moving to a new house, starting school, vacations, adoption, getting a pet—and people. The child puts the book together, drawing pictures, writing, adding clippings, photographs, mementos. Adults work with the child, filling in details and helping to ensure accuracy. You'll find that as your child works on his life book, it's a natural time to pull out those pictures, letters and other items from his birth family you've stashed away. All adopted children can gain from creating a life book, since it gives them a chance to talk about their past. Making the book also lets you talk about adoption and explore your child's knowledge and feelings.[13]

It can also include medical information on the child, anecdotes about the child, her developmental milestones, and favorite activities or hobbies.

What if your child's background includes negative information, such as alcoholism, substance abuse, or criminal activity of the birth parents? At some point your child will have questions about these matters. When you feel she is mature enough to discuss these, or when she inquires, it is your major task to emphasize to the child that she is not at fault, that she did not create the situation of her birth parents, and that she is not responsible for them. It is important also, notes Jayne Schooler, to encourage "an attitude of forgiveness. Parents should not condone or sugarcoat the behavior of birth parents. However, in an effort to avoid bitterness taking hold within the child, they can encourage the child as he matures to 'hate the sin, but forgive the sinner.'"[14]

What if you don't have much information about your child's birth parents? Holly van Gulden and Lisa Bartels-Rabb caution:

Above all, don't lie. If you don't know the answer, however, it is OK to speculate, saying something like, "Maybe your birth mother loved a boy and became pregnant. Maybe she wasn't old enough to take care of a baby. Or maybe she was very poor and couldn't buy food for you. But it must have been very hard for her when she decided she would have to let someone else take care of you." The word *maybe* is a gift from the English language for those of us who don't know the answers.[15]

Adolescents

"Teens develop their sense of who they are by seeing how they are alike and different from those who are most like them—their families."[16] This is difficult enough for biological children. Adopted teens face many additional challenges.

Wirth and Worden write:

> It may be hard for you to sort out which problems are standard adolescent difficulties and which are adoption related. It may not even make any difference. What is most important is that you continue to make home a "safe" place for your child—a place where he knows he is loved and accepted and where he can express his hurts. Encourage your child to get involved in activities where he excels and where he will meet other young people with common interests.[17]

It is especially important that your child continue to meet and talk with other adopted children. They share something that other children do not, and to be able to talk to one another about their experience can be of great benefit.

Your teen also may fantasize about her other parents. She may think they would be "more cool" or "more understanding." She may even fantasize that her birth mother was a princess who will someday return to claim her.

Rather than wanting to build a life with birth parents,

> many teenagers say that what they would really like is to be a "fly on the wall" in their birth parents' homes. They'd like to be able to observe their birth parents without being detected so they could obtain the information they want without having to be involved in the relationship.[18]

At this stage, children are becoming independent and are developing their sense of self. They will want to know all the available information. Show them their adoption papers. Let them have letters from birth mothers, if available, and anything you have that relates to their heritage.

Keep in mind:

> The desire of many adopted teenagers and adults to learn about their heritage or to meet their birth parents usually arises out of a personal need, not out of failure on the part of the adoptive parents. . . . It is important to distinguish between a real need to know and a form of quasi-searching in which adolescents go through a period of threatening their families with the idea of searching for their birth parents. This is very much like other teenagers who threaten to run away from home.[19]

Emphasize with your teenager that now *your* family has an important history together based on years of living together. This history gives her a foundation on which to build her identity.

There will perhaps come a time when your child coldly reminds you that you are not her "real parents." When and if this occurs, remember that all children sometimes make hurtful comments to their parents. One of my adopted daughters has uttered those hurtful words: "Why couldn't I be in another family?"

The child's fear of abandonment may be behind some of these reckless remarks. She was abandoned once before. Can she trust that *you* will not abandon her? These children are testing our love, and the best response is a loving response. Author Canape suggests responding, "We are your real parents and we love you. . . . But that doesn't mean that you can keep a messy room."[20] We must provide vital emotional support at this challenging time.

Searching for Birth Parents

In their search for identity, teens especially may want to know about their birth parents. Information about their birth

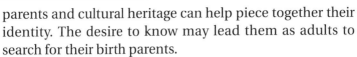

parents and cultural heritage can help piece together their identity. The desire to know may lead them as adults to search for their birth parents.

The search may have benefits for the adoptee. Jayne Schooler reports:

> A study of adopted people who had completed some portion of a birth search found that all respondents experienced considerable improvement in their lives as a result of changes brought about by their search. References to significant improvements in self-esteem, self-confidence, and assertiveness appeared frequently. Others reported that they had finally acquired feelings of connection, which had previously escaped them. Still others alluded to increased peace of mind, a sense of calmness, and a greater ability to handle and express feelings.[21]

The Logistics

After a legal adoption has been completed, the adopted child has the same legal rights as a child born into the family. The birth certificate, from that point forward, will list only the adoptive parents as parents. The original birth certificate is sealed and kept confidential.

The adoptee has no legal access to this information until he or she is an adult. Even then, only a few states allow free access by adoptees to such records. Most require the filing of a petition stating a good cause for seeking the information, and then a court appearance during which a judge grants approval or denial. "States began closing records in the 1930s to spare adoptive parents the stigma of infertility and adoptees the stigma of illegitimacy. But in today's more tolerant society, those concerns pale in favor of a sense of self-identity," says writer Troy Segal.[22]

Some states have a search and consent arrangement wherein an adoptee who would like to meet her biological parents can contact the state. The state will then contact the biological parents to see if an agreement can be reached. Still other states have a registry where the parties can register their openness and their availability. When all of the necessary parties have registered, then a meeting can be arranged.

One reason for the state's interest in adoption "reunions" is because of organ transplants in which the patient would fare better with a biologically related organ. One such case involved a man who searched for his birth mother to donate bone marrow to combat his leukemia. She was located and was willing to be a donor but insisted on her continued anonymity.[23]

Private search groups also exist. Two are Independent Search Consultants (1-714-754-7927) and The National Locator (1-800-363-FIND).

Studies have indicated that only a small percentage of adoptees actually search for their biological parents.

> When they do, they are usually between twenty-five and thirty-five years of age. It is during this age range that most adults are ready to reach a final resolution of their identity questions. The "search" is often precipitated by a major life event such as marriage, pregnancy or the birth of a child, or the death of an adoptive parent.[24]

How to Handle It

You may be tempted to ignore your child's request for help in a search or put off getting involved in the inquiry, but the best thing you can do is provide support and be involved. Lois Gilman says, "Meeting birth parents may, in fact, lead to stronger bonds between the adoptee and his adoptive parents."[25] The experience will most likely cause the adoptee to feel a deeper sense of love for the adoptive parents.

According to Jayne Schooler, "The first step that adoptive parents must take in supporting their adult child's search is to grant permission. This means letting their child know that

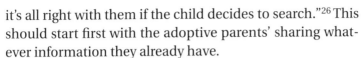

it's all right with them if the child decides to search."[26] This should start first with the adoptive parents' sharing whatever information they already have.

Adoptive parents don't have to hold their adult child's hand while she searches. You can choose your level of involvement. Your assistance may be minimal, such as checking a phone directory. Or you may choose to attend a search workshop with your child. Or you may decide to accompany her to a meeting with birth parents. Regardless of your level of involvement, a search can be a time of growth for everyone.

Don't feel threatened. Stephanie Siegel reminds us, "Whatever your children decide to do is based on who they are and not on what you did or did not do as parents."[27] If you seem to disapprove of this quest, it will only drive your child away from you. Support her and offer to help her. The prospect of your child's establishing a relationship with her birth parents has always existed, from the beginning of your adoption. If this is the result, maintain the attitude that you will all be enriched by the experience.

What if this search turns up information that is hurtful? What if the birth mother refuses to meet with your child? This is when she needs your and others' support the most. Some adoptee support groups are the American Adoption Congress, Adoptee Liberty Movement Association (ALMA), and the International Soundex Reunion Registry (see appendix A for these addresses).

How Do Adopted Children Fare?

There are volumes of research on how adopted children fare later in life. One 1985 study found that "adopted people see themselves as being more in control of their own lives and have more confidence in their own judgment than the nonadopted control group." The researchers concluded:

We have demonstrated that a study of a non-clinical population fails to show the previously suggested negative aspects of adoption. The adopted child may be different but, in contrast to the literature, may be different by being more positive rather than more negative than their nonadopted peers.[28]

This can result in positive character formation and an ability to tackle uncertainty and difficult tasks.

A study released in 1990 concluded that "teenagers adopted as infants generally have positive self-concepts, warm relationships with their parents, and psychological health comparable to that of nonadopted teens."[29] Put simply,

> Adoption is a good, and ancient way of expanding a family. It illustrates the infinite capacity of the human heart to love. No one questions the ability of a husband and wife—two who are not biologically related—to love deeply. It is no different between parent and adopted child.[30]

Strom and Donnelly note, "You can do nothing about your children's heredity, but you can do much to provide them with a positive, nurturing Christian environment. Concentrate on what you can do and trust God for the rest."[31]

Raising Biological and Adopted Children

There are many days that I reflect and ask, *How did this happen?* It is usually asked in the context of counting my many blessings. It is amusing to have gone from infertility to having three children under five years of age. On most days it is delightful. Some days I long for the peace and quiet of my single years. But I never regret our choice.

When you are raising adopted and biological children, you can't treat them all the same any more than you would treat several biological siblings the same. Each is a unique person with her own individual needs and style of interaction with you.

Lois Melina writes:

Consider that the child who is adopted may tell her sibling, "Mom and dad chose me; they had to take you." If your biological child hasn't heard you talk enthusiastically about when you were pregnant with her, she may be vulnerable to such taunts. Tell the story of your pregnancy and the child's birth with sincere joy and enthusiasm. And don't feel this has to be done outside the hearing of the child who is adopted. One mother told me that she was surprised to find her adopted children fascinated by the story of her biological child's gestation and birth. She realized it was their only chance to hear about conception, pregnancy, and birth in a personal way.[32]

I must confess that I sometimes shy away from expressing excitement over my biological child's story, particularly in front of the other children. My fear is that they will be jealous that Caitlin was in Mommy's tummy and they were in their other mommies' tummies.

One day recently, while our family was discussing our next adoption, Caitlin began to cry. When I asked her what was the matter, she said, "I'm the only one who's not adopted!" Family life, however crafted, is always interesting!

My concern about jealousy is lessened when I see the genuine love my children share. They have never teased or said any negative words about origins. I am confident they will all be lifelong friends. Perhaps this is because, while they have come to us in different ways, they are all loved with the same passion.

Keeping the Dialogue Open

Lois Melina writes:

Adoptive parents must also remember that their children can feel hurt or sad at having been placed for adoption and still be happy to be in their adoptive families, even though one wouldn't have happened without the other. Their feelings about one event may seem to conflict with their feelings about another, but they are all real emotions and need to be expressed.[33]

I believe in raising our children to be realistic and faithful. At various points in their lives, life may not make sense. They need to learn at an early age that life is sometimes difficult, that tragedies happen to good people, that some situations are unjust. If they learn these lessons early, while also learning of a faithful God who will lift them and guide them, they will not be so shaken by adult life as it unfolds.

Although we do not try to shield our children from the pain of reality, we provide them with the security of our love and the security of learning of God's love and plan for their lives. If we can instill this in their hearts at an early age, we have done a most important work, allowing them to feel good about their identity as Christians as well as adopted people.

TWELVE

Adoption and Others

n her short life, my Asian daughter has already been referred to as "flat nose" and "watermelon head." The neighborhood children have told my oldest daughter that they only play with her because she is adopted.

These realities are so painful that I want to ignore them. I wish I hadn't heard them. Yet, hard as it is, I must teach my children how to react and respond with kindness and grace to the rudeness and thoughtlessness of others. Granted, some people just don't know what to say or how to react, so they speak without thought given to the significance of their comments, but there are others, especially children, who are deliberately cruel.

Senseless and thoughtless remarks to the children are the worst, but people also make careless statements to parents: "Are they related?" referring to two Caucasian and one Asian sibling; "Where did you get them?" "Are you the baby-sitter?" The remarks bother me, but I am an adult with the ability to cope and respond. When questions or remarks are directed to innocent children, we must do something. We have an ethical duty to defend the defenseless.

People who know you, who understand your desire and motivations to raise a family, will accept your children and love them no matter how they came into the family.

If after several years and many second chances, a relative still won't accept an adopted child as a complete member of the family, parents can choose to sever contact with that relative or accept that contact with them will always be unsatisfactory. But parents can demand that the relative be respectful toward the child in his presence.[1]

A child usually cannot defend himself and so relies on knowing that the parent can and will deal with the situation. Sometimes a gentle reminder will suffice. Sometimes a humorous comment is effective. If needed, righteous indignation can be used.

Adoption expert Cheri Register says what we must do is empower our children. It is our job to begin, at a very early age, to impress on them that they have the right to choose whether, and how, to most appropriately answer intrusive questions. We empower them, but it is also our duty as parents to educate others with our words, actions, and reactions.[2]

Responding to Insensitivity

We live in a world where people say what they think and comment on things that are none of their business. It is wise to prepare your children and yourselves in advance.

Some families role-play how they will respond to the comments of others. Your school-age child could particularly benefit from this role-play when dealing with other school children. As sad as it may seem, we need to arm our children with the strength of character and the readiness of wit to face those who would judge them.

Some of the more common ridiculous things we have heard, along with our responses, are:

Comment: Isn't it wonderful of you to have taken this child in? What you're doing is admirable.

Response: What God has done in making us a family is what is admirable. His faithfulness in answering our prayers is deserving of admiration. We are the mere recipients of his blessing.

Comment: How lucky you are that you didn't have to go through the trouble of pregnancy.

Response: Nothing worthwhile in life comes without pain.

Comment to child: Do you know your real parents?

Response: Why do you want to know?

Comment to parent: Do you know the "real" parents?

Response: We are his real parents! We are a real family. Would you ever approach another parent and inquire, "Is your husband the real father of that child?" Most people wouldn't dream of it.

Comment: She looks so much like you that she could be yours.

Response: She *is* mine.

Comment: She is lucky to have you for parents.

Response: We are the lucky ones because God has blessed us with children.

Comment: You act just like a real mother!

Response: Actually, I'm a latex model of a real mother.

Comment: It takes a special person to love a child not her own. Don't you want one of your own?

Response: An adopted child is *our own.* He is our child, the one we prayed for and the one God granted to us. Would you ever ask a birth parent, "Don't you want something better than that child you have?"

Comment: Where did you get him from?

Response: God! (Unless someone is seriously inquiring about adoption, this is the best response.)

Comment: Are they sisters?

Response: Yes.

Comment: How much did that baby cost you?

This one doesn't deserve a response.

Lois Melina says, "Nobody outside the immediate family has any right or need to know the private details of the child's life or background. No parent is obliged to tell people whether the child's birth parents were married or where the child lived before the adoption."[3] She comments that this information rightfully belongs to the child and that parents do not have a right to share it with everyone who crosses their path.

Melina expresses concern that children who hear this nonresponse may conclude that their background is something to be ashamed of. Yet her greater concern is the ease with which some parents share private information with others that they have not shared with their child. The bottom line is: If your children have not been told all of the details of their history, then you do not have the right to share that information with outsiders.

Positive Adoption Language

Pat Johnston, founder of the adoption publication company Perspectives Press (see appendix D for the address), says we must use positive adoption language, or PAL. It is vocabulary that assigns the maximum respect, dignity, responsibility, and objectivity to the adoptive situation.

- The three components of adoption—the child, birth parents, and adoptive parents—are called the *adoption triad*. The allusion is to a triangle of love.
- *Special needs* is the preferred term for children with disabilities or handicaps or for children who are otherwise difficult to place.
- Overseas adoptions are referred to as *international* adoptions rather than "foreign" adoptions. The word "foreign" has too much of a negative connotation and implies something strange.

- *Asian* is the preferred term over "Oriental." "Oriental" is sometimes considered derogatory, as it is still commonly used to refer to rugs and food, but not people!
- *African American* is now the accepted term instead of "Black." Children who are of mixed race are called *biracial.*
- *Birth parents* are those who gave birth to a child. They can be called *biological parents* but should never be called "*real* parents." Adoptive parents are just as real.
- A birth child is referred to as a *biological child.* The phrase "a child of your own" should never be used, because all children in your family are your own children, regardless of how they came to be.
- A birth mother *makes an adoption plan.* This is much more neutral language than "surrender," "release," "relinquish," "give up," or "put up for adoption."
- A birth mother who keeps her child has *chosen parenting,* rather than is "keeping" her child.
- An adopted child who searches and finds birth parents *has a meeting* with them. Sometimes this is referred to as a "reunion," which is not really accurate because it implies having a shared history, which does not exist.

How we speak of adoption indicates our degree of respect and admiration and gratitude for all of the parties. The words we use will help form our children's as well as others' attitudes about adoption.

If the issue of adoption language strikes a chord with you, you might want to look into a new group called Positive Adoption Attitudes in the Media (PAAM). They were organized to react to negative adoption references on the screen and in print and to provide education to others when the subject of adoption arises. They publish a newsletter highlighting negative media portrayals and give specific advice on how to get involved (see appendix A for the address and phone number).

There is a classic little piece in adoption literature called "Four Adoption Terms Defined" by Rita Laws:

Natural child: any child who is not artificial
Real parent: any parent who is not imaginary
Your own child: any child who is not someone else's child
Adopted child: a natural child, with a real parent, who is all my own.[4]

To Tell or Not to Tell

With respect to schools, your challenge is to help your child's teacher know the child in a way that helps him learn yet does not violate his privacy or independence. If your child is of a different racial or ethnic origin, the question is simpler. Under these circumstances, children must be made to feel comfortable with adoption and not feel pressured to constantly explain themselves.

If your child looks like you, it is always an option not to tell. Our oldest daughter actually looks like me. Our biological daughter looks like my husband and the two girls look like each other. In fact, they look so much alike and are so close in age that they are often mistaken for twins. With our daughter Grace, who was born in Korea, the fact of her adoption is more obvious.

You want your child to know that adoption is a normal way for a family to come together. Not disclosing this information seems dishonest. If you value openness, what kind of message does it send to hide this information about your child from others? It is not something to be guarded and will most certainly come to light in some manner.

A preferred method to inform teachers is in a relaxed, informal way during a parent-teacher conference. If you treat adoption in a matter-of-fact way, the teacher will get the message. It is also helpful to volunteer at school to monitor classroom activities and prepare your child at home as much as possible for questions about adoption. In this way, you will also be aware of places in the curriculum where your child will be forced to deal with the adoption issue, and you can help him through it.

Instructions to bring unavailable baby photos to school, family tree assignments, or the genetic studies in biology classes that highlight your child's missing links are common curriculum features that would need special treatment. An alternative to bringing baby photos might be to have your child draw himself when he was younger, then draw himself as he is now. The point of this exercise is usually to show the growth of the child, and this can be shown by drawing. Younger children who are given the family tree assignment can use the family tree of their adoptive family. Next to their name, they may want to add the date that they joined the family. The point of this exercise is usually to teach children about family relationships, such as identifying the degree of relationship between cousins, aunts, and grandparents. Older elementary children who are asked to do this assignment will want to begin to fill in the details of their biological heritage to show how race, ethnicity, and physical features are passed from generation to generation.

If you want to become substantially involved, you may offer to conduct a teacher workshop or a culture day for your child's class. You may work on your local or district level to encourage some space in the curriculum to explore adoption. You may want to donate some of your adoption books to your school. You could arrange to have an adoption expert talk to your child's class, or have someone come in to talk about your child's ethnic heritage.

Many local support groups have materials on adoption awareness. These materials offer suggestions on school programs, letters to write to libraries asking them to stock adoption literature, and other helpful suggestions.

 THIRTEEN

Open versus Closed Adoption

N ot long ago, closed adoptions were the norm. The adoption process and participants were shrouded in secrecy. In recent years, changes in adoption procedures have brought about "open" adoptions and even "cooperative" adoptions. "Open" or "closed" refers to the extent of information or contact exchanged between adoptive and birth parents. This chapter takes a close look at these differences.

Closed Adoption

The "closing" of adoptions was common in the United States by the 1930s. It was thought that such a practice would allow both birth parents and child the opportunity to have a fresh start in life. In a closed adoption, privacy is assured by legal edict.

In the traditional closed adoption, the baby is relinquished by the birth mother and placed through an agency or attorney with an adoptive family. Neither parents are told much about the other. Birth parents and adoptive parents may exchange some nonidentifying information such as medical and social histories. Where an intermediary exists, such as an agency or attorney, this information is typically shared in writing. Often in the rush and delight of an adoption, the information is shared verbally, sometimes third- or fourth-hand. As you learn information, try to remember to write it down at some point so it is not lost in the excitement. You may never have access to such information in the future.

When we adopted our first child, we received verbal information from the hospital social worker. She promised a written report later but claimed she lost the information. Thankfully, I remember most of what she told us, but not all. She had specifically interviewed our birth mother about her likes, dislikes, and personal history. It has been fun to share that information with our daughter as she grows older.

Kay Strom and Douglas Donnelly comment:

> While many children have been placed into wonderful and loving homes, critics charge that the closed adoption system treated the birth mother as a non-person and was insensitive to the needs of many adoptees to know, "Who am I, really?" It was in response to these concerns that open adoption developed.[1]

Because a relationship is created in which the past does not exist, participants in a closed adoption are not given a chance to resolve the many issues of loss associated with adoption. As adoption professionals began to measure the benefit of the "clean-break" theory of privacy, they concluded that it was far outweighed by the potential damage of secrecy. Changes in our societal attitude toward illegitimacy helped create a climate that was ready for openness in adoption.

There are three inherent problems in closed adoption.

Open versus Closed Adoption

1. Guilt and grief felt by the birth mother. Open adoption allows her resolution of some issues, since she knows that her child is doing well and being well cared for by adoptive parents.
2. A lack of information received by adoptive parents. Open adoption allows them to have accurate details about their child's background.
3. The adoptees' need to know their identity. Open adoption permits adoptees to know their history and come to terms with their genetic identity. They do not have to pretend they had no history before the adoption and they can move beyond the sense of rejection that can accompany traditional adoption.

Open Adoption

If the concept of open adoption is confusing it is because there is no agreement on a definition. Some refer to an open adoption as one in which all the parties meet and have a continuing relationship. Some refer to an open adoption as one in which the adoptive parents are "open" in communicating about the adoption with their child. Others refer to an open adoption as one in which the birth parents select adoptive parents and may have a series of meetings prior to the birth with contact in writing thereafter. For our purposes, an open adoption is one in which there is some contact among the members of the adoption triad.

Open adoption was initially popularized by the publication of the book *The Adoption Triangle* (1979) by A. D. Sorosky, Annette Baran, and Reuben Pannor. This group of social workers believed that closed adoptions were destructive by their secrecy. The first open adoptions took place in the late 1970s and the number skyrocketed in the 1980s and 1990s.

The Degree of Contact

The degree of contact, either in person or by letter, runs the gamut from very little to extensive. In most open adoptions, there is a great deal of contact around the time of placement, but it often diminishes over time. In some open adoptions, there may be a single meeting. In others there may be a deep, long-standing friendship. The relationship can be structured to meet the needs and desires of the adoption triad.

Regardless of the degree of openness promised, most adoptive parents will send photos and updates for at least the first year of the child's life. Contact tends to be most frequent during that year. After a year, the birth mother is generally getting on with her life, perhaps marrying or finishing school or having other children. There are no legal obligations or contractual arrangements that may force adoptive parents to maintain contact or that could affect the finalization of the adoption. A reliance is placed on the good will of the parties to honor their agreements to stay in contact.

If you are pursuing adoption with an agency that advocates open adoptions, make sure you are clear how they define openness. How much contact is to be expected? If you are not comfortable with what the agency recommends, this may not be your best option.

Some Advantages

Although the positive benefits of open adoption have not been proven empirically, some preliminary studies are encouraging. Researchers from the School of Social Work at the University of Texas at Austin analyzed the perspective of the birth mothers, the parents, and the children themselves in open adoptions.

Of birth mothers who had meetings and an exchange of information with the adoptive couple, most "expressed feelings of happiness during the meetings because they felt assured that their decision was the right one or they derived satisfaction from the delight of the adoptive parents." Adoptive parents expressed two major concerns. First, they were concerned that they would not be able to control the birth family's involvement in their family's life. Second, they feared that the birth mother would try to reclaim the child as her own. The study, however, showed that "the overwhelming majority of adoptive parents across all levels of openness indicated satisfaction with their ability to control such involvement." Further, fears that the birth mother would want to reclaim the child were lessened because the adoptive parents had formed first-hand impressions of the birth parents and about their life circumstances and had heard first-hand their own statements about the adoption decision. Regarding the children themselves, the researchers stated that "virtually all of the children, no matter what type of adoption they had, wanted to know more about their birth parents."[2]

This study concludes that adoptive openness is not a single event but rather an ongoing process. The relationships that seem to work best are those that evolve mutually and gradually. Semi-open adoptions, in which there is minimal contact between the parties, seem to be the best for all concerned. They allow the greatest benefit and the least risk.

An open adoption gives a child permission to care about both sets of parents. "With the birth parent only a letter or telephone call away, there's also less reason to fantasize about his other parents," notes Lois Gilman. "They are real people whose likes and dislikes he knows. As for his adoptive parents, he has a 'sense of belonging' since he is aware that his birth parents chose them for him."[3] In a sense, adoptive parents are freer to parent and bond with the child because they have been empowered and entrusted by the birth parents with their blessings.

What if the birth parent chooses to diminish contact? How do you explain this to the child? Gilman warns:

> It is . . . important for the adults choosing to create an open adoption to understand its long-range emotional impact on the child. Even if your child's birth parents stop writing or calling you after four or five years, you've got to continue to be in contact with them—even if it's just a brief note—for your child's sake. At a later point your child will be able to make his own decision about the nature of the ongoing relationship.[4]

The following beliefs on the part of adoptive parents will increase the likelihood of a successful open adoption.

- Children have a right to know who they are and how they joined their families and to grow up knowing the truth.
- Children do not cease to have a connection with their birth family because they are adopted. They have a right to information about their birth family and to maintain a connection with them.
- Children have a right to be recognized by society as full and equal members of their adoptive families.
- Children have a right to freely ask questions and express their feelings about being adopted.
- Children have the right to be accepted as individuals with a unique genetic heritage that is modified, enhanced, and developed by the environment in which they are raised.
- Children have a right to a positive sense of racial identity as well as a positive sense of family identity.
- Families have the right to choose the circumstances under which they disclose to others their involvement in adoption.
- Being placed for adoption is a separate issue from being adopted. Being infertile is a separate issue

from being an adoptive parent. Having an unwanted pregnancy is not the same as not wanting the child. Each has a separate emotional reaction.[5]

If these statements ring true to you, then open adoption may be for you.

Cooperative Adoption

New adoptive arrangements are being tested to meet the desires of birth mothers. One such arrangement is called a cooperative adoption.

Cooperative-adoption counselor Sharon Kaplan defines cooperative adoption as "the child's access to both families, to both sets of parents, with progressive participation in the decisions that will affect his other life."[6]

Strom and Donnelly note:

> The distinction between "open" and "cooperative" adoption is this: With whom does the birth mother have a relationship? If her relationship is with the adoptive parents only, it is an open adoption. If her relationship is with the child as well, then it is a cooperative adoption. The critical distinguishing feature of cooperative adoption is that the birth parent(s) have the right to visit with the child after the adoption is final.[7]

This practice is extremely controversial. Criticism falls into three major areas: first, this arrangement amounts to co-parenting; second, it is too confusing for the child to sort out all these relationships; and finally, it may interfere with the adoptive parents' ability to cement a bond with their child because of the continuing presence of the birth parent(s).

Adoptive couples who are likely to succeed with this arrangement have to be mature and able to set limits on the birth parent's involvement. Without maturity and boundaries, a cooperative adoption could result in bitterness for everyone involved.

Some Reasons for Caution

Open adoption is not without problems. Because of its relative newness, more research needs to be done on whether it is best for the children involved.

Many adoptive couples are not comfortable with openness. You should not proceed if you don't feel at ease with any aspect of an open adoption. Complete honesty with your feelings is owed to your child, the birth parents, and yourselves.

A 1990 paper by a team of social workers with St. Mary's Services, a child welfare agency in Chicago, concludes:

> For birth mothers open adoption is a complex and sometimes deceptive choice, leading to a relationship for which there is no social precedent. Sometimes a young birth mother hopes to find in the adoptive parents a new set of parents for herself. Often she expects to have a role in the family, like that of an aunt, a sister, a godmother or a baby-sitter, and doesn't face the fact that she has given up a child.
>
> For adoptive parents, the study found, open adoption can hinder "any healthy parent's capacity to form a secure and comfortable close bond with an infant." And for an adopted child there are risks of "serious interference" at every stage of his development. An open adoption is likely to leave him feeling like a foster child, with no sense of permanence in his adoptive family and to force him to reckon with his adopted status abruptly and prematurely when it is best for him to assimilate this fact gradually over time.[8]

Open adoption has unfolded in a manner perhaps unintended by its originators, social workers Annette Baran and Reuben Pannor. It is used now by lawyers and agencies as a marketing tool to attract birth mothers who wish to exercise a great deal of control over the placement of their child. The focus was formerly on finding homes for homeless children. Now the focus is on providing children for childless couples. It is a subtle but substantial shift. Baran comments, "What has happened is that the entrepreneurs, motivated by profit, have insinuated themselves into the open-adoption system. They are empathetic but into business."[9]

If you are contemplating an open adoption, make sure all the expectations are clearly defined and understood by all the parties.[10]

 FOURTEEN

The Future

t is hard to be an adoptive parent and not be an advocate for adoption. Every time I speak to someone who is interested in adoption, I am advocating adoption. When I educate someone about international adoption, I am advocating adoption. When I can sensitively and intelligently respond to an insensitive remark about adoption, I am advocating adoption.

Some adoptive parents become more active than this. A support group that is committed to public education is one way to increase acceptance of adoption. Many support groups are actively involved in public education and awareness programs. When you reach the point of being a proud adoptive parent, it will be natural to share your joy and enthusiasm for adoption.

Author Charlene Canape says, "The adoptive couples and their adopted children who love each other and enjoy their lives together are the best advertisement ever for adoption."[1] What could be a more positive picture of adoption than being a happy, healthy, emotionally balanced family? Yet the media focus in the last few years has been on the cases that are an adoptive parent's worst nightmare.

The Headline Cases

Who can forget the anguished cries of the children in the cases of disrupted adoption that were in the news? Baby Jessica and Baby Richard haunt the minds of all adoptive parents.

Although these cases garnered intense media interest and tugged at the hearts of all parents, they are rare. Of the approximately fifty thousand private adoptions that take place in this country each year, less than 1 percent are contested by birth parents who seek the return of a child, according to the National Council for Adoption. In the comparatively minute number of cases that do go awry, problems could have been predicted nearly from the beginning.

Armed with insufficient information about these cases, the public tends to be eager to place blame on one side or the other. In fact there is enough blame to go around, with a healthy dose of blame to be heaped on the lumbering legal system itself, which allows these battles to drag on over the precious years of childhood.

Jessica DeBoer, now known as Anna Jacqueline Schmidt, was ordered returned to her biological parents after living with Jan and Roberta DeBoer for more than two years. In this case, Cara Schmidt, the birth mother, did not provide the correct name of the birth father. The DeBoers, ignorant of her deception, accepted the child and began legal proceedings to adopt her.

Within a month, Cara Schmidt reconciled her relationship with Dan Schmidt, the true birth father, and they were ultimately married. Each filed papers to have the child returned to them on the basis that rights of the true birth father had never been terminated.

After two-and-one-half years of legal wrangling, the then-preschooler was returned to her birth parents. Although the adoption tangle started with the exposed lie of the birth mother, it was compounded by the adoptive parents' continuing refusal to recognize that their adoption was unraveling for them.

In the Illinois Baby Richard case, the deception runs even deeper. The birth mother (Daniela Kirchner), believing that the birth father had jilted her for an old girlfriend, informed the birth father (Otakar Kirchner) that the baby had died. The birth parents reconciled, and Daniela informed Otakar on Mother's Day of 1991 that the child had been placed for adoption. Some eighty days after the birth and placement of the child, Mr. Kirchner challenged the case in court. Although Mr. Kirchner was well beyond Illinois's thirty-day window of opportunity in which a birth father is compelled to assert a claim, he successfully argued that he could not stake a claim to a child he did not know was alive.

The boy had never met his biological father. Yet at four years of age, he was taken from the home of Kim and Bob Warburton, his adoptive parents, and placed in the permanent custody of his biological parents. Although visitation was promised to the Warburtons, to date they have not seen the little boy. His brother has not been allowed to visit the sibling who lived with him for over four years.

I am always near tears when I view television footage of Baby Richard when he was "transferred" to his biological parents. One writer described it this way: "The event . . . is referred to by all concerned as 'the transfer'—much as one might speak of funds being shifted from a savings account to an IRA."[2] As of this date, the Kirchners have separated, and Baby Richard is in the sole custody of the woman who initially used him as a pawn to ensnare the birth father. What will become of this child?

There were several danger signs in both cases, chiefly having to do with birth fathers. One way to address this issue is to ensure the birth mother receives counseling. If her decision is made in a lawyer's office with no outside advice, and if the birth father is not involved in the decision-making process, her consent may not be reliable.

Another danger sign for any adoption case is the birth father who is unknown or cannot be located. Although most states provide some type of notification process for such birth fathers, this method of securing consent is not reliable. Coupled with possible deception on the part of the birth mother, the birth father's absence produces a formula for disaster.

In each high-profile case, adoptive parents learned of snags in the adoption relatively early on. They denied the seriousness of the situation and tenaciously stood by their children. "Why do adoptive parents ignore obvious precautions? In a word: desperation," notes writer Michelle Ingrassia.[3]

Recent cases may be attributable to the publicity given recently to the rights of birth fathers. Some fathers, now aware of their rights, are willing to challenge an adoption. Because termination and finalization of adoption orders are subject to appeal, many cases have been dragged out to preserve birth fathers' rights. This is complicated by a lack of uniformity of adoption laws from state to state: Some allow independent adoption; some allow only agency adoption.

Additionally, the American social welfare system has always operated on the assumption that it is best for the child to keep a biological family together. Thus a child who could clearly benefit from a permanent placement may be shuttled back and forth from foster care or a potential adoptive home to the birth parent if the birth parent shows even the slightest effort to take responsibility for the child. People who adopt abandoned, abused, or neglected children often find themselves childless again when the birth parents realize that they are permanently losing their child.

Some Possible Solutions

I am a belt-and-suspenders kind of person. I go to extremes to make certain all my bases are covered so that I can

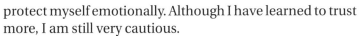

protect myself emotionally. Although I have learned to trust more, I am still very cautious.

I believe, therefore, that adoptive families should be prepared, prior to the placement of a child, with an answer to the question, What if the birth parents change their minds? If a birth parent changes his or her mind early on in the proceeding, you are in for tremendous grief if you should choose to resist. This is the position of a cautious person. I do not wish to rely on legislation or the courts to support my emotional position. I believe it is best for adoptive parents to be prepared for the worst and rejoice in the best. I also believe there are changes our society could make that would help the cause of adoption.

To Prevent Failure

Reconsider proceeding. If a birth father cannot be found or refuses to consent, adoptive parents should proceed with caution. One need only remember the anguish of all of the parties in the Baby Jessica and Baby Richard cases to see why this is crucial.

Establish birth father registries. As I mentioned in a previous chapter, some states have established birth father registries where a man can register his paternity. Before a court terminates any father's rights, the state must consult this registry. This also keeps the adoptive parents from having to track down the birth father. Already fourteen states have established such data banks: Arizona, Arkansas, Georgia, Idaho, Illinois, Indiana, Iowa, Louisiana, Missouri, New Mexico, New York, Oklahoma, Tennessee, and Utah.

This policy presumes much about human nature. It presumes that birth fathers will rush to declare their paternity when they learn of an unwanted pregnancy. It presumes everyone wants to cooperate in the notification process. Although it does not address all of the problems, it is a partial solution.

Consider the child's interest. Illinois has adopted legislation proposed by Governor James Edgar in response to the Baby Richard case allowing courts to consider the best interest of the child in contested adoption cases. I support this legislation. Yet I am concerned that it will be improperly used by adoptive parents to delay court challenges for months and months. By the sheer passage of time and the interminable delay of court proceedings, they may then claim that it is in the best interest of the child to stay with the adoptive family when the birth mother has made it clear early on that she made a mistake in placing her child.

Consider other similar safeguards. The law in Illinois provides some other new safeguards for adoptive parents. In addition to the birth father registry, the birth mother must also provide information about the birth father's identity, and any false statements she makes in this regard are considered to be a crime and are punishable as a Class B misdemeanor. If a birth father has not registered his interest in the child, he may not later contest any adoption proceeding with regard to that child. *A lack of knowledge of the pregnancy or birth is not an acceptable reason for failure to register.*

Make laws uniform. A uniform adoption act could be considered by state legislatures. As it stands now, states vary widely in their requirements for taking consents and for setting time limits during which those consents can be challenged. Most proposals would prohibit a final adoption from being challenged more than six months after finalization and would also allow the child's welfare to be taken into consideration in contested adoptions. Uniform laws are difficult for individual states to accept. Each wants to maintain autonomy in legislation. Achieving the agreement of fifty states on adoption law is a noble goal. At minimum, it is a point of discussion.

Insist on complete information. There are no implicit or explicit warranties on adoptions. Laws governing the amount of information an adoptive parent can receive about a child's background vary from state to state. If the adoption is independent, there may be even less information. An agency will usually interview the birth parents, but a lawyer doing an independent adoption may not. There should be uniformity in the quantity and quality of information available to adoptive parents, and full information should be freely available, where possible. This would address the very few cases of fraud where adoptive parents seek to rescind their adoptions because of some undisclosed negative information from the agency. This is called Wrongful Adoption.

Act swiftly. Social service agencies should act swiftly in making decisions about the future of the children in their care. Many children languish in foster care, neither being cared for by their own families nor being made available for adoption. By the time many of these children are free for adoption, their age or acquired emotional problems make them less desirable candidates. Decisions about termination of parental rights should be made without delay. Until then, agencies should encourage foster-adoption relationships, whereby the foster parents would have the first option to adopt a child who is freed for adoption.

To Encourage Adoption

Seek out birth mothers. All agencies should more aggressively seek out unwed mothers. Unprepared birth mothers need to know that there is an alternative to abortion or single parenting. Whether agencies advertise or rely on extensive word of mouth and community education, they need to make sure that unwed mothers know what options are available to them before making their final decision. The successful private agencies are those that actively recruit birth mothers, adequately counsel them, and responsibly place the children.

Consider birth mothers. Agencies also need to be more sensitive to the needs of a birth mother. This can be as simple as offering to meet her in a neutral setting (other than a formal office) or allowing her to play a more active role in choosing the family for her placement. This is one area that is improving rapidly. Often now birth mothers can play an active role in the selection of adoptive parents in even the most conservative agency.

Counseling. Birth mothers who choose adoption should receive thorough counseling, which does not happen in many private adoptions. Lawyers are essentially in a business relationship with their clients and are often unprepared to secure counseling for birth mothers. If this is not addressed by legislation, it should at least be addressed by attorney bar associations.

Provide aid. More financial assistance should be made available for adoptive parents. Medical insurance carriers would not go broke by paying the birth mother's expenses under the coverage of the adoptive parents' policy. Corporations could provide nominal stipends toward the cost of adoption. Adoptive parents should receive the same paid parental leave as birth parents. Many have to take personal leave to bond with their new child. Where adoptive parents are allowed to take parental leave, equal financial benefits should be afforded the newly formed family.

Some Predictions

Michael R. Sullivan makes several predictions about adoption in the late 1990s and beyond.

- The imbalance in the supply and demand of readily available healthy newborns will continue. This may be affected by the success of efforts to restrict abortion.
- The trend toward more private adoptions will increase, as will numbers of international adoptions.

- Adoptions will not become any easier. There will be much more costly litigation as we sort out what is best for the children.
- Birth parents will have more options in the adoption planning process. Birth mothers, who want input into the placement of their baby, will be attracted by private adoptions. Birth fathers will become more involved in the process. The open adoption trend will continue.
- Costs will continue to increase. These include medical and legal expenses, housing and living expenses, counseling, transportation, and post-placement counseling expenses.[4]

Other issues the states will have to grapple with are whether the government support of unwed mothers is cost-effective and whether everyone would benefit from the states' subsidizing adoptions for adoptive families. The debate is likely to linger for another generation.

The Adoptee's Bill of Rights

Lois Melina proposes seven rights that all adopted children should enjoy. This is a great beginning point of discussion for anyone touched by adoption—the children, all parents, adoption workers, and those in the legal system. As you consider these rights, you will be formulating your own approach to adoptive parenting—one based on a strong foundation of love, acceptance, commitment, and honesty.

1. Children have the right to know who they are and how they joined their families, and to grow up knowing the truth.
2. Children have a right to freely ask questions and express their feelings about being adopted.

3. Children have a right to a positive attitude about their birth parents.
4. Children have the right to be accepted as individuals with a unique genetic heritage.
5. Children have a right to be recognized by society as full and equal members of their adoptive families.
6. Information about our children's origins is private information that belongs to them.
7. Transracially adopted children have a right to a positive sense of racial or ethnic identity.[5]

 **FIFTEEN**

God's Adopted Children

Our families on earth are temporary. Our pastor says we're just walking about in our earth suits. In heaven, we will forsake these suits for heavenly garb. The thing that will endure is our adoption into God's family.

Raising adopted children has been a wonderful opportunity to express to our children this concept of our adoption into God's family. The Bible instructs, "In love he predestined us to be adopted as his sons through Jesus Christ" (Eph. 1:4–5). Scripture speaks of adoption as a perfect, permanent love relationship. No better model exists for our families.

Biblical Examples of Adoption

Jesus is a prime example of an adopted child. He was not Joseph's biological son. Joseph was his earthly father. God was his heavenly Father.

Stories of adoption abound in the Old Testament as well. Two of the stories your children will learn early in their lives are those of Moses and Samuel.

Moses' mother put him in a basket to be discovered and "adopted" by Pharaoh's daughter. His mother cleverly arranged circumstances to remain serving as the child's nurse. She could see her son grow but could no longer claim him as her own. Even though Moses was born a Hebrew, his adoption by Pharaoh's daughter meant that he was now legally entitled to all civil and religious rights of an Egyptian. His past was severed and a new identity found in his adoptive family.

Likewise Hannah prayed for a child and was given a son named Samuel. She surrendered him to the priest Eli in fulfillment of the promise she made to God. In essence, Eli "adopted" Samuel to train him in the service of the Lord.

Our Family and God's Family

When we receive Christ in our lives, we become sons and daughters of God by the Spirit of adoption. Romans 8:15–16 reads, "For you did not receive a spirit that makes you a slave again to fear, but you received the Spirit of sonship. And by him we cry, 'Abba, Father.' The Spirit himself testifies with our spirit that we are God's children." When we are adopted as God's sons (Eph. 1:5), we make a break with past relationships and forge a new, permanent relationship with the Lord. The Lord tells us, "I will be a Father to you, and you will be my sons and daughters" (2 Cor. 6:18). It is a new relationship, a beginning. Our adoption as God's children parallels the adoption of our earthly children into our families.

When your child is old enough to begin the discussion about adoption, you can use this wonderful truth to help him understand his position as an adopted child in your earthly family and in the family of God. Just as it was God's will to send that child to your home, it is God's will that we,

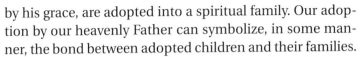

by his grace, are adopted into a spiritual family. Our adoption by our heavenly Father can symbolize, in some manner, the bond between adopted children and their families.

Our adoption by our heavenly Father is based in love. "How great is the love," the Bible says, "the Father has lavished on us, that we should be called children of God!" (1 John 3:1). I often reflect on the greatness of his love when I count the blessings he has bestowed on me in the form of my children. How great is that love that I am his child and that he has entrusted others of his children into my care!

"Each adoption story is its own small miracle," say authors Wirth and Worden. "Many adoptive families feel the power of God more intensely than at any other time in their lives. They sense that God is arranging things for them and their children in a way that transcends human logic and power."[1]

Each of our children was a direct, unexpected, undeserved gift of grace. I have prayed the prayer of a barren woman and my prayer has been answered abundantly. Such blessings have only strengthened personal faith and fanned the fire of desire to tell others of the goodness of our God.

Our Children Are Not Our Own

Our children are not our property. They belong to God. We are given the job of raising and training them while they are on the earth.

This is helpful for us to remember at all stages in the adoption process. God determines whether you will raise children. If you do raise children, they will inevitably grow up and leave you. If you remember that they are always subject to God's influence, this will make their coming or going, their health or misfortune, easier for you to bear. If you entrust them into God's care at an early age, you and your children can share in this confidence.

Children are a reward from the Lord (Ps. 127:3). We are their caretakers on earth. But their heavenly Father watches over them constantly and eternally. He is a "father of the fatherless" (Ps. 68:5) and has a plan for each of us.

"'For I know the plans I have for you,' declares the LORD, 'plans to prosper you and not to harm you, plans to give you hope and a future'" (Jer. 29:11). It is our charge, in the short time our children are with us, to encourage them in their love and knowledge of the Lord so that their lives will be a tribute to a gracious God.

Epilogue

The Bible tells us: "Children are a reward from [the LORD]. Blessed is the man whose quiver is full of them" (Ps. 127:3, 5). I never thought I would have children. I don't know why the Lord has blessed me so!

A Tribute to Our Children

Clare: You came to us when I was in despair. God had taken a biological pregnancy, leaving me depressed and hopeless. When I heard you would be coming home with us, I was ecstatic. You helped to mend my broken heart. I began to believe that our love was to be shared and that we would have input into the next generation. We showered you with love and attention, never guessing that your love would start a chain reaction of children in our home!

Caitlin: You came to us as a shock. You were one of God's surprises, showing us his sense of humor in our lives. We weren't ready for you, but you made us ready to love you. You continue to be a source of surprise and delight.

Grace: You came to us as a pure expression of God's love when we had reason to question his plan for our lives. You have kept us excited about parenting. Your sweetness shines through the stressful days and reminds us that childhood consists of such moments of sunshine and grace—if we will only take the time to appreciate them.

To our child who may arrive: You will be the conclusion of a chapter in our lives and the opening of a whole new book. We haven't raised a boy and we are thrilled beyond belief at the prospect of training up a man whose life will glorify God.

You are each an undeserved reward from the Lord. We humbly accept his graciousness and seek to raise you according to his will.

A Letter to Our Birth Mothers

You are the women who gave birth to Clare, to Grace, and to our future son. Words cannot express our gratitude for your sacrifice. I often think about you and when I do, gratitude wells up in my heart. I was barren, and you filled my house with children. How can I ever repay you?

When we pray together as a family, we remember each of you. We pray that you will know peace. We pray that you will feel that your decision was a good one because your child is cherished in our home.

We acknowledge your sadness, and we hope you can feel blessed by our gratitude. If you could somehow touch the joy we feel at being the parents of your child, you would rejoice with us as well. You have done a selfless thing that will not go unrewarded. Our two oldest daughters remind us that we will all be together in heaven—birth mothers, birth fathers, half siblings, deceased grandparents—all of us who choose to embrace the love and forgiveness of God. This is our prayer for each of you, as well as for all of us.

 APPENDIX A

Adoption Associations, Parent and Adoptee Support Groups, and Resources

ome of these listings are reprinted here with the permission of Adoptive Families of America. They are taken from their excellent publication *AFA's Guide to Adoption*.

AASK America
(Adopt A Special Kid, America)
657 Mission St., Ste. 601
San Francisco, CA 94105
1-800-23-AASK-1; 415-543-2275
Maintains registries of special needs children and prospective families. No fees charged.

Adoptee Liberty Movement Association (ALMA)
P.O. Box 154
Washington Bridge Station
New York, NY 10033
212-581-1568
An adoptee support group.

Adoptive Families of America
3333 Highway 100 North
Minneapolis, MN 55422
612-535-4829; 1-800-372-3300 to subscribe to the magazine.
Fax: 612-535-7808
Supports, educates, and advocates on behalf of all kinds of adoption-built families. Publishes the bimonthly magazine *Adoptive Families*, sells essential adoptive parenting resources, has a twenty-four-hour help line, provides a national conference, and more.

Alliance of Genetic Support Groups
1001 22nd St. NW, Ste. 800
Washington, DC 20037
1-800-336-GENE; 202-331-0942
A national coalition of genetic support groups, concerned individuals, and professionals. Increasing awareness of genetic disorders.

American Academy of Adoption Attorneys
Box 33053
Washington, DC 20033-0053
Attorneys making independent adoption a part of their legal practice. Write for a free directory.

American Adoption Congress
1000 Connecticut Ave. NW
Washington, DC 20036
1-800-274-6736
An adoptee support group.

American Public Welfare Association
810 First St. NE, Ste. 500
Washington, DC 20002-4267

The CAP Book
700 Exchange St.
Rochester, NY 14608
716-232-5110
Publishes a frequently updated national photo-listing book of U.S. children who wait for adoptive families and can be placed across state lines.

Child Welfare League of America, Inc.
440 First St. NW, Ste. 310
Washington, DC 20001
202-638-2952

Provides consultation, training programs, and conferences; conducts research; publishes books and pamphlets; and advocates on behalf of children. Its Library Information Service offers films, slide shows, and cassette tapes on various adoption issues.

Committee for Single Adoptive Parents
Box 15084
Chevy Chase, MD 20815
Provides helpful information for United States and Canadian singles interested in adoption opportunities and publishes a single adoptive parent handbook.

Immigration and Naturalization Service
Director, Outreach Program
425 I St.
Washington, DC 20536
Publishes *The Immigration of Adopted and Prospective Adoptive Children*, a guide to the entrance requirements for international children.

International Concerns Committee for Children
911 Cypress Dr.
Boulder, CO 80303
303-494-8333
Offers information on adoptable domestic and foreign children, has an overseas orphanage sponsorship program, and publishes an annual *Report on Foreign Adoption*. Also matches waiting children with prospective families.

International Soundex Reunion Registry
P.O. Box 2312
Carson City, NV 89702-2312
702-882-7755
Provides a registry for all members of the adoption triad to register their willingness to be in contact with one another.

LaLeche League International
1400 N. Meacham Road
P.O. Box 4079
Schaumburg, IL 60168-4079
1-800-LALECHE
Write to them for information about breast-feeding an adopted infant.

National Adoption Center
1500 Walnut St., Ste. 701
Philadelphia, PA 19102
1-800-TO-ADOPT
Fax: 215-735-9410

Offers general adoption information, a bibliography of books on adoption for children and youth, and a newsletter. Also offers computer matching of waiting children and prospective adoptive families.

The National Adoption Foundation
100 Mill Plain Road
Danbury, CT 06811
203-791-3811
Provides some grant funding for adoption. Also makes referrals to lenders who loan funds specifically for adoption.

National Adoption Information Clearinghouse
11426 Rockville Pike, Ste. 410
Rockville, MD 20852
301-231-6512
Provides information about all aspects of adoption, including adoption publications, referrals to adoption-related services, searches of its computerized information databases, and copies of state and federal laws relating to adoption.

National Foster Parent Association
226 Kilts Dr.
Houston, TX 77024
713-467-1850
Provides information, encouragement, and support for foster families.

National Resource Center for Special Needs Adoption
Spaulding for Children
16250 Northland Dr., Ste. 120
Southville, MI 48075
313-443-7080
Publishes books on adoption issues and refers parents to agencies and health professionals with expertise in special needs adoption.

North American Council on Adoptable Children
970 Raymond Ave. #106
St. Paul, MN 55114-1149
612-644-3036; 1-800-470-6665 for adoption subsidy questions only.
Focuses on the needs of waiting U.S. and Canadian children. Provides legislative advocacy, research, and policy analysis; the quarterly newsletter *Adoptalk*; grants for the development of replicable local training and support services, and an annual national conference.

PAAM
P.O. Box 15293
Chevy Chase, MD 20825
202-244-9092
Positive Adoption Attitudes in the Media was organized to react to negative media coverage about adoption and to provide education about adoption. Write for a newsletter and further information.

Resolve, Inc.
310 Broadway
Sommerville, MA 02144
617-623-0744
Provides services for couples dealing with a fertility impairment. Offers adoption information, education, referral, and support.

Single Parents for Adoption of Children Everywhere (SPACE)
6 Sunshine Ave.
Natick, MA 01760
Offers an annual conference specifically for single adoptive parents and singles seeking to adopt.

Stars of David International, Inc.
3175 Commercial Ave., Ste. 100
Northbrook, IL 60062-1915
708-205-1200
Fax: 708-205-1212
A nonprofit information and support network for Jewish and partly Jewish adoptive families.

 APPENDIX B

Selecting a Private Agency or Attorney

Finding a Private Agency

Agencies may be located through several sources. Your state child welfare office will have a list of local agencies. Adoptive Families of America's extensive pamphlet, *AFA's Guide to Adoption*, is regularly updated and has the most current information about agencies across the country. The pamphlet includes details about the types of adoptions the agencies handle, the costs, and requirements (see appendix A for the address).

The *AFA's Guide to Adoption* will help you get started on your search. Each agency handles different types of cases. Some may be accepting applications, some may not. Before working with any agency, check its references and licensing status. Talk to other parents who have used its services.

Questions for Any Agency

1. What types of children does your agency work with?
2. What countries do you work with?

3. How many children a year are placed through your agency?
4. What ages are the children that you place?
5. What are your requirements for age of adoptive parents, length of marriage, income, or religion?
6. (If applicable) Will your agency work with families who already have a child or children?
7. Do you have information sessions for prospective parents? When?
8. How much does a typical domestic adoption cost? What is the waiting time?
9. How much does a typical international adoption cost? What is the waiting time?
10. Does your agency do home studies? What is involved in that process?
11. What is the charge for a home study?
12. Can we have references of families who have adopted through you in the last two years?
13. Do you have parent support groups?
14. Has your agency had any adoptions fail in the past two years? Why?
15. What do we do next if we want to pursue adoption through your agency?

Questions for Special Needs Agencies

In addition to the questions above, you will want to ask special needs agencies the following:

1. How do children with special needs come to your agency? Are they all legally ready to be adopted?
2. Do you have a foster-adoption program? (The foster parents will be considered first for adoption when and if the child becomes legally free for adoption.)
3. Can we receive counseling to help us choose the kind of child we can work with?
4. Can you help us look for financial aid before *and* after placement of a child?
5. What post-adoption services do you offer?
6. Do you offer respite care to adoptive families?
7. Can you give us the names of parents who have adopted children with special needs through your agency in the past two years?

Questions for an Attorney

1. What will your role be in the adoption process? (Will you merely provide leads to birth mothers or will you actively secure a potential birth mother for us?)
2. What methods do you employ to find birth mothers?
3. Do you advocate open adoption? How much confidentiality will be preserved?
4. What is your experience? How many adoptions have you done in each year of your practice? Do you have a list of clients available whom I may contact?
5. What percentage of your adoptions fall through?
6. How much will this cost? Do you charge a flat fee or an hourly rate? What is the average cost for an adoption, from start to finish, including all filing fees and costs? What would be the additional fees if the adoption is contested at some point?
7. Is a retainer required? How much is it?
8. What will happen to fees or a retainer paid if the adoption falls through?
9. How do you stay in contact with adoptive parents? Will someone in your office keep us updated if you are not available?
10. Will you be the intermediary to accept phone calls from birth mothers at your office? Who will screen the birth mothers and how will this be done?
11. Will you encourage the birth parents to receive counseling and help them receive it? What counselors do you work with?

A Directory of Adoption Attorneys

The following list is provided with the permission of the American Academy of Adoption Attorneys, an association of attorneys who make independent adoption a part of their practice. The author and publisher do not recommend or advocate any particular attorney. Ask each for references of other families they have assisted. Check their license status with the local attorney registration authority. Talk to other adoptive parents before selecting any professional to assist you. A geographical listing of these attorneys begins on page 204.

Abrams, Lauren J.
3395 Willard St.
San Diego, CA 92122
Office: 619-453-9135
Fax: 619-457-2792

Albers, James S.
88 North Fifth St.
Columbus, OH 43215
Office: 614-464-4414
Fax: 614-442-2617

Allen, Maryon A.
631 Beacon Pkwy. West #102
Birmingham, AL 35209
Office: 205-290-0077
Fax: 205-290-0758

Allison, Gary B.
1092 Laskin Road #112
Virginia Beach, VA 23451
Office: 804-422-1212
Fax: 804-428-5753

Amrhein, Richard J.
70 East Beau St.
Washington, PA 15301
Office: 412-222-4520
Fax: 412-222-3318

Anderson, G. Darlene
105 North Rose St. #200
Escondido, CA 92027
Office: 619-743-4700
Fax: 619-743-6218

Andrel, Vika
3908 Manchaca Road
Austin, TX 78704
Office: 512-448-4605
Fax: 512-448-1905

Appell, Cheryl Linda
10 Alcorn Ave. #306
Toronto, Ontario
Canada M4V 1E4
Office: 416-927-0891
Fax: 416-927-0385

Arnett, Carolyn S.
One Riverfront Plaza #1708
Louisville, KY 40202
Office: 502-585-4368
Fax: 502-585-4369

Azulay, Daniel
35 E. Wacker Dr.
Chicago, IL 60601
Office: 312-236-6965
Fax: 312-236-1805

Badger, Jeffrey Ewen
P.O. Box 259
Salisbury, MD 21803-0259
Office: 410-749-2356
Fax: 410-749-8731

Bado, Barbara K.
1800 Canyon Park Circle #301
Edmond, OK 73013
Office: 405-340-1500
Fax: 405-340-1780

Bado, John Terry
1800 Canyon Park Circle #301
Edmond, OK 73013
Office: 405-340-1500
Fax: 405-340-1780

Ball, Teresa L.
2800 Patterson Ave. #100
Richmond, VA 23221
Office: 804-358-6669
Fax: 804-358-5290

Barnette, David Allen
P.O. Box 553
Charleston, WV 25322-0553
Office: 304-340-1327
Fax: 304-340-1380

Bates, Gerald A.
500 Throckmorton St. #1404
Fort Worth, TX 76102
Office: 817-338-2840
Fax: 817-338-2865

Batt, Lawrence I.
209 S. 19th St. #400
Omaha, NE 68102-1757
Office: 402-346-2000
Fax: 402-346-4108

Bauer, Martin W.
300 Page Ct., 220 W. Douglas
Wichita, KS 67202
Office: 316-265-9311
Fax: 316-265-2955

Baum, David H.
16255 Ventura Blvd. #704
Encino, CA 91436-2302
Office: 818-501-8355
Fax: 818-501-8465

Bayliss, Barbara
4525 Wilshire Blvd. #201
Los Angeles, CA 90010
Office: 213-664-5600
Fax: 213-664-4551

Beck, Mary
206 Hulston Hall
Columbia, MO 65211
Office: 314-882-7872
Fax: 314-884-4368

Bell, Richard C.
4401 Belle Oaks #250
Charleston, SC 29405
Office: 803-554-1103
Fax: 803-554-3580

Beltz, W. Thomas
316 N. Tejon St.
Colorado Springs, CO 80903
Office: 719-473-4444
Fax: 719-444-0186

Bender, Rita L.
1301 Fifth Ave., 34th Floor
Seattle, WA 98101
Office: 206-623-6501
Fax: 206-447-1973

Berman, Jeffrey
5830 Hubbard Dr.
Rockville, MD 20852
Office: 301-468-1818
Fax: 301-881-7871

Berry, Judith M.
28 State St.
Gorham, ME 04038
Office: 207-839-7004
Fax: 207-839-8250

Blackmore, Margaret L.
536 South High St.
Columbus, OH 43215
Office: 614-221-1341
Fax: 614-228-0253

Blied, Timothy J.
4100 Newport Place Dr. #800
Newport Beach, CA 92660-
2422
Office: 714-863-1644
Fax: 714-863-0164

Bluestein, Craig
200 Old York Road
Jenkintown, PA 19046
Office: 215-576-1030
Fax: 215-576-5380

Bluestein, Craig B.
One Greentree Center #201
Marlton, NJ 08054
Office: 609-988-5513

Bostick, Shelley Ballard
20 North Wacker Dr. #3710
Chicago, IL 60606
Office: 312-541-1149
Fax: 312-629-5499

Boydston, Karla Jill
2300 Hemphill
Fort Worth, TX 76110
Office: 817-922-6010
Fax: 817-926-8505

Brail, Herbert A.
930 Mason St.
Dearborn, MI 48124
Office: 313-278-8775
Fax: 313-278-3602

Bremyer-Archer, Jill
P.O. Box 1146
McPherson, KS 67460-1146
Office: 316-241-0554
Fax: 316-241-7692

Appendix B

Brewer, Susan M.
P.O. Box 768
Southaven, MS 38671-0768
Office: 601-342-6000
Fax: 601-342-6031

Bricker, Harry L., Jr.
407 North Front St.
Harrisburg, PA 17101
Office: 717-233-2555
Fax: 717-233-8555

Broome, David P.
1408 1st Nat. Bank Bldg.
P.O. Box 1944
Mobile, AL 36633-1944
Office: 205-432-9933
Fax: 205-432-9706

Brown, C. Harold
500 Throckmorton #3030
Forth Worth, TX 76102-3817
Office: 817-338-4888
Fax: 817-338-0700

Brust, Jennifer
2000 N. 14th St. #100
Arlington, VA 22201
Office: 703-525-4000
Fax: 703-525-2207

Buchanan, Paul M.
P.O. Box 3375
Nashville, TN 37219-0375
Office: 615-256-9999
Fax: 615-726-1494

Butler, Cynthia Calibani
2109 Cache Road, C
Lawton, OK 73505
Office: 405-248-1511
Fax: 405-248-1565

Callahan, Ellen Ann
12600 War Admiral Way
Gaithersburg, MD 20878
Office: 301-258-2664
Fax: 301-258-2665

Casey, Barbara L. Binder
527 Elm St., P.O. Box 399
Reading, PA 19603
Office: 610-376-9742
Fax: 610-376-6783

Chally, John
825 NE Multnomah #1125
Portland, OR 97232
Office: 503-238-9720
Fax: 503-239-3989

Charney, Mitchell A.
3000 National City Tower
Louisville, KY 40202
Office: 502-589-4440
Fax: 502-581-1344

Clark, Mary W.
10 Eighth St. S.E.
Paris, TX 75460
Office: 903-785-0391
Fax: 903-785-6688

Cobb, Deborah Crouse
6100 Center Grove Road #5
Edwardsville, IL 62025-3301
Office: 618-692-6300
Fax: 618-692-9831

Cohn, Bennett S.
205 6th St.
West Palm Beach, FL 33401
Office: 407-833-8747
Fax: 407-833-5997

Collopy, Michael J.
P.O. Box 2297
Hobbs, NM 88241-2297
Office: 505-397-3608
Fax: 505-397-1379

Cook, D. Durand
8383 Wilshire Blvd. #1030
Beverly Hills, CA 90211
Office: 213-655-2611
Fax: 213-852-0871

Appendix B

Coppock, S. Dawn
2101 Doane Lane
Strawberry Plains, TN 37871
Office: 615-933-8173
Fax: 615-933-3272

Copps, Anne Reynolds
279 River St. P.O. Box 1530
Troy, NY 12181
Office: 518-272-6565
Fax: 518-272-5573

Cox, Heidi Bruegel
2300 Hemphill
Fort Worth, TX 76110
Office: 817-922-6043
Fax: 817-926-8505

Crockin, Susan L.
One Gateway Center #601 West
Newton, MA 02158
Office: 617-332-2020
Fax: 617-244-2835

Cubbage, William R.
P.O. Box 550
Cushing, OK 74023-0550
Office: 918-225-2464
Fax: 918-225-7292

Daulton, David T.
125 St. Paul's Blvd. #600
Norfolk, VA 23510-2708
Office: 804-640-7777
Fax: 804-640-0156

Davis-Loomis, Nancy
Master in Chancery
Circuit Court
Anne Arundel County
Annapolis, MD 21404-2395
Office: 410-222-1284
Fax: 410-268-9762

Demaray, Mark
1420 5th Ave. #3650
Seattle, WA 98101-2387
Office: 206-682-4000
Fax: 206-682-4004

DeSmidt, Jody O.
701 4th Ave. South #650
Minneapolis, MN 55415-1606
Office: 612-340-1150
Fax: 612-340-1154

Dexter, Catherine M.
921 Southwest Washington
  #865
Portland, OR 97205
Office: 503-222-2474
Fax: 503-274-7888

Donnelly, Douglas R.
926 Garden St.
Santa Barbara, CA 93101
Office: 805-962-0988
Fax: 805-966-2993

Donohue, Sara M.
200A Monroe St. #315
Rockville, MD 20850
Office: 301-294-0460
Fax: 301-294-6406

Dubin, Steven G.
101 Washington Lane #110
Jenkintown, PA 19046
Office: 215-885-1210
Fax: 215-885-1217

Eckman, Mark L.
404 Pine St. #202
Vienna, VA 22180
Office: 703-242-8801
Fax: 703-242-8804

Eisenman, Susan G.
338 South High St.
Columbus, OH 43215
Office: 614-222-0540
Fax: 614-222-0543

England, Les F.
3760 S. Highland Dr. #500
Salt Lake City, UT 84106-4206
Office: 801-278-7755
Fax: 801-273-3912

Essig, Ellen
105 East Fourth St. #900
Cincinnati, OH 45202
Office: 513-721-5151
Fax: 513-621-9285

Fahlman, Robert James
201-919 Fort St.
Victoria, British Columbia
Canada V8V 3K3
Office: 604-388-4931
Fax: 604-386-8088

Feeney, Peter J.
P.O. Box 437
Casper, WY 82602
Office: 307-266-4422
Fax: 307-237-5030

Ferguson, R. A., Jr.
290 21st St. North #600
Birmingham, AL 35203
Office: 205-251-2823
Fax: 205-251-3832

Finn, Robert W.
1988 N. Kalb
Tucson, AZ 85715
Office: 602-722-0185

Fishbein, Rhonda
17 Executive Park #480
Atlanta, GA 30329
Office: 404-248-9205
Fax: 404-248-0419

Flam, Joan
16133 Ventura Blvd. #700
Encino, CA 91436-2440
Office: 818-986-6840
Fax: 818-784-0827

Fleischner, Robin A.
11 Riverside Dr. #14 MW
New York, NY 10023
Office: 212-362-6945
Fax: 212-875-1431

Fleischner, Robin A.
159 Millburn Ave.
Millburn, NJ 07041
Office: 201-376-6623
Fax: 212-875-1431

Flint, Robert B.
717 K St.
Anchorage, AK 99501
Office: 907-276-1592
Fax: 907-277-4352

Fox, Debra M.
355 West Lancaster Ave.
Haverford, PA 19041
Office: 215-896-4832
Fax: 215-896-4834

Franke, Carolyn Mussio
3411 Michigan Ave.
Cincinnati, OH 45208
Office: 513-871-8855
Fax: 513-871-8897

Franklin, Gregory A.
95 Allens Creek Road, Bldg. 1
  #104
Rochester, NY 14618
Office: 716-442-0540
Fax: 716-442-6889

Friedman, Herbert D.
115 Broad St., 6th Floor
Boston, MA 02110
Office: 617-451-0191
Fax: 617-451-2580

Gapen, Carol M.
P.O. Box 1784
Madison, WI 53701-1784
Office: 608-256-0226
Fax: 608-259-2601

Garvert, Melinda L.
2606 Fleming #6
Garden City, KS 67846
Office: 316-275-2300
Fax: 316-275-0730

Garvert, Melinda L.
3617 Betty Drive, G
Colorado Springs, CO 80917
Office: 719-591-0093
Fax: 719-596-0352

Gawron, Steven L.
2850 Metro Drive #429
Bloomington, MN 55425
Office: 612-854-4483
Fax: 612-854-2103

Ginsburg, Julie E.
60 Walnut St.
Wellesley, MA 02181
Office: 617-237-8630
Fax: 617-237-5272

Gitlin, H. Joseph
111 Dean St.
Woodstock, IL 60098
Office: 815-338-0021

Glass, Todd I.
330 East Main St. #4
Muncie, IN 47305
Office: 317-288-0207
Fax: 317-286-0816

Gleason, Sharon L.
360 K St.
Anchorage, AK 99501
Office: 907-276-5231
Fax: 907-278-6328

Goldheim, Laurie B.
1 Blue Hill Plaza
Pearl River, NY 10965
Office: 914-735-9650
Fax: 914-620-0761

Goldman, Elisabeth
118 Lafayette Ave.
Lexington, KY 40502
Office: 606-252-2325
Fax: 606-252-2325

Goldstein, Michael S.
62 Bowman Ave.
Rye Brook, NY 10573

Office: 914-939-1111
Fax: 914-939-2369

Gorman, Jane A.
930 West 17th St., D
Santa Ana, CA 92706
Office: 714-558-1099
Fax: 714-285-9895

Gradstein, Marc
1204 Burlingame Ave. #7
Burlingame, CA 94010-4126
Office: 415-347-7041
Fax: 415-347-7048

Grammer, Susan
P.O. Box 111
Bethalto, IL 62010-0111
Office: 618-259-2113
Fax: 618-259-2003

Greenberg, Karen K.
144 Gould St.
Needham, MA 02194-3063
Office: 617-444-6611
Fax: 617-449-3093

Gustafson, J. Eric
222 North 3rd St.
Yakima, WA 98901
Office: 509-248-7220
Fax: 509-575-1883

Gutterman, Tara E.
3900 City Line Ave. #A-603
Philadelphia, PA 19131
Office: 215-844-1082
Fax: 215-842-9881

Hardesty, Theresa Rahe
7513 North Regent Place
Peoria, IL 61614
Office: 309-692-1087
Fax: 309-692-5334

Hassen, John R.
129 N. Oakdale
Medford, OR 97501
Office: 503-779-8550
Fax: 503-773-2635

Hawley, John T., Jr.
1087 West River #230
Boise, ID 83702
Office: 208-343-8880
Fax: 208-345-0314

Hayes, Stephen W.
411 E. Wisconsin Ave.
Milwaukee, WI 53202
Office: 414-276-1122
Fax: 414-276-6281

Hazlett, Allan A.
1608 S.W. Mulvane St.
Topeka, KS 66604-2746
Office: 913-232-2011
Fax: 913-232-5214

Herman, Flory
338 Harris Hill Road #110
Williamsville, NY 14221
Office: 716-631-9971
Fax: 716-631-9973

Herrin, John Q.
3400 Bank One Center Tower
Indianapolis, IN 46204-5134
Office: 317-636-3551
Fax: 317-636-6680

Hester, Jerrold W.
3941 Holcomb Bridge Road
  #200
Norcross, GA 30092
Office: 404-446-3645
Fax: 404-840-9725

Hicks, Randall B.
6608 Palm Ave.
Riverside, CA 92506
Office: 909-369-3342
Fax: 909-682-2531

Hinz, Michele Gentry
1420 5th Ave. #3650
Seattle, WA 98101-2387
Office: 206-682-4000
Fax: 206-682-4004

Hirschfeld, John C.
P.O. Box 6750
Champaign, IL 61826-6750
Office: 217-352-1800
Fax: 217-352-1083

Hodgkinson, Terry L.
10303 Jasper Ave. #1200
Edmonton, Alberta
Canada T5W OK9
Office: 403-421-9900
Fax: 403-421-4151

Hodgson, Sandra L.
825 N.E. Multnomah #1125
Portland, OR 97232
Office: 503-238-9720
Fax: 503-239-3989

Horder, Richard A.
1100 Peachtree St. #2800
Atlanta, GA 30309-4530
Office: 404-815-6538
Fax: 404-815-6555

Hubert, Timothy J.
P.O. Box 1287
Evansville, IN 47706-1287
Office: 812-426-1231
Fax: 812-464-3676

Hultquist, Allen C.
707 Broadway #1100
San Diego, CA 92101
Office: 619-233-3000
Fax: 619-233-3016

Ivers, Larry E.
221 West Broadway, P.O. Box C
Eagle Grove, IA 50533
Office: 515-448-3919
Fax: 515-448-5251

Johnson, Dale R.
7303 Blanco Road
San Antonio, TX 78216
Office: 210-349-3761
Fax: 210-349-9373

Johnson, Jerry M.
400 West North St.
Lima, OH 45801
Office: 419-222-1040
Fax: 419-227-1826

Jones, Barbara C.
5265 O'Faly Road
Fairfax, VA 22030
Office: 703-278-8072
Fax: 703-278-8022

Kahn, Lawrence A.
10711 Cambie Road #270
Richmond, British Columbia
Canada V6X 3C9
Office: 604-270-9571
Fax: 604-270-8282

Kalos, Carolyn
62 Bowman Ave.
Rye Brook, NY 10573
Office: 914-939-1111
Fax: 914-939-2369

Kaye, Jeffrey M.
14 Beacon St. #616
Boston, MA 02108
Office: 508-682-4413
Fax: 617-227-6308

Keefe, Catherine W.
120 South Central #1505
Clayton, MO 63105
Office: 314-727-7050
Fax: 314-727-3467

Kelley, Eugene T.
222 West Walnut St.
Rogers, AR 72756
Office: 501-636-1051
Fax: 501-636-1663

Kirsh, Joel D.
401 Pennsylvania Pkwy. #370
Indianapolis, IN 46280-1390
Office: 317-575-5555
Fax: 317-575-5631

Kirsh, Steven M.
401 Pennsylvania Pkwy. #370
Indianapolis, IN 46280-1390
Office: 317-575-5555
Fax: 317-575-5631

Klima, Robert H.
9257 Lee Ave. #201
Manassas, VA 22110
Office: 703-361-5051
Fax: 703-330-2090

Klockau, Lori L.
402 South Linn
Iowa City, IA 52240
Office: 319-338-7968
Fax: 319-354-4871

Krigel, Sanford P.
900 Harzfeld Bldg.
1111 Main St.
Kansas City, MO 64105
Office: 816-474-7800
Fax: 816-474-9390

Kunin, Israel L.
612 S. 10th St.
Las Vegas, NV 89101
Office: 702-384-8489
Fax: 702-384-8464

Kuster, Ann McLane
2 Capital Plaza, P.O. Box 1500
Concord, NH 03302-1500
Office: 603-226-2600
Fax: 603-228-2294

Lackmeyer, Michael R.
1201 South W. S. Young Dr.
Killeen, TX 76543
Office: 817-690-2223
Fax: 817-699-4324

Lane, Karen R.
100 Wilshire Blvd. #2075
Santa Monica, CA 90401
Office: 310-393-9802
Fax: 310-393-5071

Leavitt, David Keene
9454 Wilshire Blvd., Penthouse
Beverly Hills, CA 90212
Office: 310-273-3151
Fax: 310-273-5452

Lesko, Deborah L.
5032 Buttermilk Hollow Road
West Mifflin, PA 15122
Office: 412-469-3500
Fax: 412-469-0289

Leventon, Martin
355 West Lancaster Ave.
Haverford, PA 19041
Office: 610-642-3322
Fax: 610-642-7731

Lewin, Stephen
845 Third Ave. #1400
New York, NY 10022
Office: 212-759-2600
Fax: 212-593-1318

Lifshitz, Richard A.
120 North LaSalle St. #2900
Chicago, IL 60602
Office: 312-236-7080
Fax: 312-236-0781

Linkner, Monica Farris
3250 Coolidge Highway
Berkley, MI 48072
Office: 810-548-1430
Fax: 810-546-8858

Lirhus, Albert G.
2200 6th Ave. #1122
Seattle, WA 98121
Office: 206-728-5858
Fax: 206-728-5863

Loker, Mary G.
30 E. Padonia Road #404
Timonium, MD 21093
Office: 410-561-3000
Fax: 410-560-0588

Loomis, Laurie A.
1001 Bishop St.
1300 Pacific Tower
Honolulu, HI 96813-3544
Office: 808-524-5066
Fax: 808-531-3553

Lowell-Britt, Denise
30 West First St.
Mesa, AZ 85201
Office: 602-461-5300
Fax: 602-461-5398

Lowndes, Thomas P.
128 Meeting St.
Charleston, SC 29401
Office: 803-723-1688
Fax: 803-722-7439

Lyons, Beth Marietta
28 North Florida St.
Mobile, AL 36607
Office: 205-476-7857
Fax: 205-476-8510

McDermott, Mark T.
1300 19th St. N.W. #400
Washington, DC 20036
Office: 202-331-1955
Fax: 202-293-2309

Macias, Richard
622 North St. Francis Ave.
Wichita, KS 67214-3810
Office: 316-265-5245
Fax: 316-265-3953

McIntyre, Linda W.
10239 West Sample Road
Coral Springs, FL 33065
Office: 305-344-0990
Fax: 305-344-0997

Mackin, Paula
1 Prescott St.
Charlestown, MA 02129-3711
Office: 617-242-1689
Fax: 617-242-1689

McLeod, Kaye Hartenstein
620 West Third St. #210
Little Rock, AR 72201
Office: 501-372-1121
Fax: 501-376-9614

Magovern, Frederick J.
111 John St. #2509
New York, NY 10038-3001
Office: 212-962-1450
Fax: 212-385-0235

Maricic, George
800 N. Haven Ave. #440
Ontario, CA 91764
Office: 909-945-9549
Fax: 909-980-5525

Meckler, Cynthia Perla
83 Blue Heron Ct.
Buffalo, NY 14051
Office: 716-688-1540
Fax: 716-886-2720

Meiser, Rita
2 N. Central #1600
Phoenix, AZ 85004
Office: 602-262-5841
Fax: 602-253-3255

Mesberg, Christine
28 Hilltop Road
Waccabuc, NY 10597
Office: 914-669-5401
Fax: 914-669-8105

Meyer, Ellen S.
521 West St.
Wilmington, DE 19801
Office: 302-429-0344
Fax: 302-429-8806

Michelsen, Diane
3190 Old Tunnel Road
Lafayette, CA 94549-4133
Office: 510-945-1880
Fax: 510-933-6807

Milner, Lisa
P.O. Box 23059
Jackson, MS 39225-3059
Office: 601-948-6100
Fax: 601-355-6136

Miroff, Franklin I.
251 East Ohio St. #1000
Indianapolis, IN 46204
Office: 317-264-1040
Fax: 317-264-1039

Miskowski, James
45 N. Broad St.
Ridgewood, NJ 07450
Office: 201-445-4600
Fax: 201-612-0715

Modica, Michele M.
2 Kilburn St.
Revere, MA 02151
Office: 617-286-4936
Fax: 617-286-2859

Moffet, Susan C.
921 Southwest Washington
   #865
Portland, OR 97205
Office: 503-222-2474
Fax: 503-274-7888

Morris, Edith H.
1515 Poydras St. #1870
New Orleans, LA 70112
Office: 504-524-3781
Fax: 504-561-0228

Morrison, Kathleen Hogan
120 North LaSalle St. #2900
Chicago, IL 60602
Office: 312-236-7080
Fax: 312-236-0781

Moyer, Darlis E.
1 Court Square, P.O. Box 1368
Harrisonburg, VA 22801-1368
Office: 703-434-9947
Fax: 703-434-9865

Musgrave, Dawn Oxley
6 Sudbrook Lane
Baltimore, MD 21208
Office: 410-486-9020
Fax: 410-653-2764

Mushkin, Rhonda
930 S. 3rd St. #300
Las Vegas, NV 89101
Office: 702-386-3999
Fax: 702-388-0617

Myers, Scott E.
3180 East Grant Road
Tucson, AZ 85716
Office: 602-327-6041
Fax: 602-326-9097

Newton, Judith Sperling
P.O. Box 1784
Madison, WI 53701-1784
Office: 608-256-0226
Fax: 608-259-2600

Nichols, Suzanne
11 Martine Ave.
White Plains, NY 10606
Office: 914-949-7755
Fax: 914-949-8305

Nichols, Suzanne
420 Chestnut St.
Union, NJ 07083
Office: 908-964-1096
Fax: 908-964-1098

Nunez, Linda
513 E 1st St., 2nd Floor
Tustin, CA 92680-3339
Office: 714-544-9921
Fax: 714-544-5155

O'Brien, Rosemary G.
109 South Fairfax St.
Alexandria, VA 22314
Office: 703-549-5110
Fax: 703-684-0843

O'Shea, Brendan C.
11 North Pearl St.
Albany, NY 12207
Office: 518-432-7511
Fax: 518-432-5221

Painter, David
P.O. Box 1586
Lake Charles, LA 70602
Office: 318-436-1415
Fax: 318-436-2403

Paquet, Susan I.
1701 River Run Road #1021
Fort Worth, TX 76107
Office: 817-338-4854
Fax: 817-338-9127

Peck, Susan
3190 Old Tunnel Road
Lafayette, CA 94549-4133
Office: 510-945-1880
Fax: 510-933-6807

Petty, Jack H.
6666 N.W. 39th Expwy.
Bethany, OK 73008
Office: 405-787-6911
Fax: 405-787-6913

Phillips, Betsy H.
Route 4, Box 179-P
Rustburg, VA 24588
Office: 804-821-5022
Fax: 804-821-6092

Phillips, Stanton E.
2009 N. 14th St. #510
Arlington, VA 22201
Office: 703-522-8800
Fax: 703-841-0845

Pidgeon, Kathryn A.
8433 N. Black Canyon Hwy
  #100
Phoenix, AZ 85021-4859
Office: 602-371-1317
Fax: 602-371-1506

Poole, Rodney M.
2800 Patterson Ave. #100
Richmond, VA 23221
Office: 804-358-6669
Fax: 804-358-5290

Poster, Nancy D.
9909 Georgetown Pike, P.O.
  Box 197
Great Falls, VA 22066
Office: 703-759-1560
Fax: 703-759-6512

Price, Susan Beth
26 W. Dry Creek Circle #520
Littleton, CO 80120
Office: 303-347-2004
Fax: 303-347-2788

Printz, Jane G.
1717 Louisiana N.E. #103
Albuquerque, NM 87110
Office: 505-262-1671
Fax: 505-255-4029

Queal, Irv W.
8117 Preston Road #600
Dallas, TX 75225-6306
Office: 214-373-9100
Fax: 214-373-6688

Quinn, Colleen Marea
823 East Main St., 16th Floor
Richmond, VA 23204
Office: 804-644-1440
Fax: 804-225-8706

Radis, David J.
1901 Ave. of the Stars, 20th
  Floor
Los Angeles, CA 90067
Office: 310-552-0536
Fax: 310-552-0713

Randall, Ross S.
3112 Brockway Road, P.O. Box
  1287
Waterloo, IA 50704-1287
Office: 319-235-9507
Fax: 319-233-8041

Rees, Natalie H.
409 Washington Ave. #920
Baltimore, MD 21204-4903
Office: 410-494-8080
Fax: 410-494-8082

Reiniger, Douglas H.
630 Third Ave.
New York, NY 10017-6705
Office: 212-972-5430
Fax: 212-972-5835

Rosen, William P., III
Station Square Three #202
Paoli, PA 19301
Office: 610-647-8800
Fax: 610-647-2080

Rosenstock, Lucille
4480 N. Osage Dr.
Tucson, AZ 85718
Office: 602-529-1005
Fax: 602-577-0735

Rosin, Benjamin
630 Third Ave.
New York, NY 10017-6705
Office: 212-972-5430
Fax: 212-972-5835

Royall, Donald R.
13430 Northwest Frwy. #650
Houston, TX 77040
Office: 713-462-6500
Fax: 713-462-6570

Royall, Melody Brooks
13430 Northwest Frwy. #650
Houston, TX 77040
Office: 713-462-6500
Fax: 713-462-6570

Sacharow, Steven B.
950 Kings Hwy. N., Box 8484
Cherry Hill, NJ 08002-0484
Office: 609-667-1111
Fax: 609-779-8850

Sapp, Susan Kubert
1900 Firstier Building
Lincoln, NE 68508
Office: 402-474-6900
Fax: 402-474-5393

Schaffer, Peter K.
204 North Robinson #2600
Oklahoma City, OK 73102
Office: 405-239-7707
Fax: 405-239-7709

Scherer, Mary Ann
2734 E. Oakland Park Blvd.
#200
Fort Lauderdale, FL 33306
Office: 305-564-6900
Fax: 305-564-0187

Scherr, Leslie
815 Connecticut Ave. N.W.
#500
Washington, DC 20006
Office: 202-785-2168
Fax: 202-828-5393

Schroeder, Victoria J.
383 Williamstowne
Delafield, WI 53018
Office: 414-646-2054
Fax: 414-646-2075

Shelander, Mel W.
245 North Fourth St.
Beaumont, TX 77701
Office: 409-833-2165
Fax: 409-833-3935

Shorstein, Michael A.
1660 Prudential Dr. #402
Jacksonville, FL 32207
Office: 904-348-6400
Fax: 904-348-6424

Shrybman, James A.
801 Wayne Ave. #400
Silver Spring, MD 20910
Office: 301-588-0040
Fax: 301-495-9104

Sifferman, Kelly A.
7000 N. 16th St. #120-419
Phoenix, AZ 85020
Office: 602-997-8831
Fax: 602-331-1122

Silberberg, Amy M.
15511 Afton Hills Dr. South
Afton, MN 55001
Office: 612-228-1455
Fax: 612-224-7754

Smith, Mary E.
711 Adams St.
Toledo, OH 43624
Office: 419-243-6281
Fax: 419-243-0129

Smoot, Carolyn
208 North Market, P.O. Box
1234
Marion, IL 62959
Office: 618-993-2700
Fax: 618-993-5042

Solomon, Toby
354 Eisenhower Pkwy.
Livingston, NJ 07039
Office: 201-533-0078
Fax: 201-533-0466

Somit, Jed
1440 Broadway #910
Oakland, CA 94612
Office: 510-839-3215
Fax: 510-839-7041

Spiegel, Laurence H.
4040 SW Douglas Way
Lake Oswego, OR 97035
Office: 503-635-7773
Fax: 503-635-1526

Steffas, Irene A.
4187 Kindlewood Ct.
Roswell, GA 30075-2686
Office: 404-642-6075
Fax: 404-587-3475

Steincolor, Deborah
281 Liberty St.
Bloomfield, NJ 07003
Office: 201-743-7500
Fax: 201-748-4836

Steincolor, Deborah
845 Third Ave. #1400
New York, NY 10022
Office: 914-429-1000

Stewart, Allan F.
120 S. Central #1505
Clayton, MO 63105
Office: 314-727-7050
Fax: 314-727-3467

Stockham, Susan L.
2520 South Tamiami Trail
Sarasota, FL 34239
Office: 813-957-0094
Fax: 813-957-0084

Stocks, Janis K.
1450 Frazee Road #409
San Diego, CA 92108
Office: 619-296-6251
Fax: 619-296-6315

Stoddart, Ronald
1698 Greenbriar Lane #201
Brea, CA 92621
Office: 714-990-5100
Fax: 714-671-7834

Stulting, Janet S.
68 South Main St.
W. Hartford, CT 06127
Office: 203-561-4832
Fax: 203-521-5560

Swaim, James E.
318 West Fourth St.
Dayton, OH 45402
Office: 513-223-5200
Fax: 513-223-3335

Swain, Margaret E.
21 W. Susquehanna Ave.
Towson, MD 21204
Office: 410-823-1250
Fax: 410-296-0432

Swanson, Cynthia Stump
500 E. University Ave., C
Gainesville, FL 32601
Office: 904-375-5602
Fax: 904-373-7292

Tanenbaum, Allan J.
359 E. Paces Ferry Road #400
Atlanta, GA 30305
Office: 404-266-2930
Fax: 404-231-3362

Tenenbaum, Joel D.
3200 Concord Pike, P.O. Box
  7329
Wilmington, DE 19803
Office: 302-477-3200
Fax: 302-477-3210

Thaler, Carolyn H.
29 W. Susquehanna Ave. #205
Towson, MD 21204
Office: 410-828-6627
Fax: 410-296-3719

Thompson, Fletcher D.
P.O. Box 1853
Spartanburg, SC 29304
Office: 803-573-7575
Fax: 803-585-0183

Thompson, James Fletcher
P.O. Box 1853
Spartanburg, SC 29304-1853
Office: 803-573-7575
Fax: 803-585-0183

Thornton, Megan Lake
163 West Short St. #300
Lexington, KY 40507
Office: 606-231-8780
Fax: 606-231-6518

Thurman, W. David
801 East Trade St.
Charlotte, NC 28202
Office: 704-377-4164
Fax: 704-377-5503

Totaro, Samuel, Jr.
3325 Street Road #100
Bensalem, PA 19020
Office: 215-244-1045
Fax: 215-244-0641

Townes, W. Waverley
730 West Main St. #500
Louisville, KY 40202
Office: 502-583-7400
Fax: 502-589-4997

Tuke, Robert D.
201 Fourth Ave. North #1700
Nashville, TN 37219
Office: 615-313-3300
Fax: 615-313-3310

Uram, Susan W.
230 Villard Ave.
Hastings-on-Hudson, NY 10706
Office: 914-478-5971
Fax: 914-478-5971

Vader, Joseph N.
P.O. Box 1185
Olathe, KS 66051
Office: 913-764-5010
Fax: 913-764-5012

Vargas, Noel E., II
526 Rue St. Louis #302
New Orleans, LA 70130
Office: 504-561-8129
Fax: 504-561-8182

Vincent, Judith D.
111 Third Ave. South #240
Minneapolis, MN 55401
Office: 612-332-7772
Fax: 612-332-1839

Walling, Wright S.
701 4th Ave. #650
Minneapolis, MN 55415
Office: 612-340-1150
Fax: 612-340-1154

Washburn, Michael C.
10330 Regency Parkway Dr.
Omaha, NE 68114
Office: 402-397-2200
Fax: 402-390-7137

Webster, Felice
4525 Wilshire Blvd. #201
Los Angeles, CA 90010
Office: 213-664-5600
Fax: 213-664-4551

Weinman, Ellen S.
15 South College Ave.
Salem, VA 24153-3833
Office: 703-389-3825

Weith, Glenna J.
P.O. Box 6750
Champaign, IL 61826-6750
Office: 217-352-1800
Fax: 217-352-1083

Wexell, Richard M.
3975 University Dr. #410
Fairfax, VA 22030
Office: 703-385-3858
Fax: 703-385-9652

Whitmire, Bryant A., Jr.
215 N. 21st St.
Birmingham, AL 35203
Office: 205-324-6631
Fax: 205-324-6632

Widelock, Marc D.
5401 California Ave. #300
Bakersfield, CA 93309
Office: 805-325-6950
Fax: 805-325-7882

Wiernicki, Peter J.
1300 19th St. N.W. #400
Washington, DC 20036
Office: 202-331-1955
Fax: 202-293-2309

Wildman, Sally
180 North LaSalle #2401

Chicago, IL 60601
Office: 312-726-9214
Fax: 312-782-4033

Wilson, Elizabeth Karsian
401 Locust St. #406, P.O. Box
  977
Columbia, MO 65205-0977
Office: 314-443-3134
Fax: 314-442-6323

Worcester, Nanci R.
210 Magnolia Ave. #2
Auburn, CA 95603
Office: 916-888-1311
Fax: 916-823-3299

Wright, Brinton D.
P.O. Box 3112
Greensboro, NC 27402-3112
Office: 910-373-1500
Fax: 910-272-8258

Yacobi, Stephen A.
408 N. Church St., B
Greenville, SC 29601
Office: 803-242-3271
Fax: 803-233-3750

Yarell, Ellen A.
1980 Post Oak Blvd. #1720
Houston, TX 77056
Office: 713-621-3332
Fax: 713-621-3669

Zimmerman, Golda
117 S. State St.
Syracuse, NY 13202-1103
Office: 315-475-3322
Fax: 315-475-7727

Zimmerman, Phyllis L.
15 W. 6th St. #1220
Tulsa, OK 74119-5444
Office: 918-582-6151
Fax: 918-582-6153

Ziskin, Daniel I.
3309 North Second St.

Phoenix, AZ 85012
Office: 602-234-2280
Fax: 602-234-0013

Zuflacht, Linda M.
8703 Wurzbach Road
San Antonio, TX 78240
Office: 512-699-6088
Fax: 512-691-8836

Geographical Listing

Alabama
Allen, Maryon A.
Broome, David P.
Ferguson, R. A., Jr.
Lyons, Beth M.
Whitmire, Bryant A., Jr.

Alaska
Flint, Robert B.
Gleason, Sharon L.

Arizona
Finn, Robert W.
Lowell-Britt, Denise
Meiser, Rita A.
Myers, Scott E.
Pidgeon, Kathryn A.
Sifferman, Kelly A.
Ziskin, Daniel I.

Arkansas
Kelley, Eugene T.
McLeod, Kaye H.

California
Abrams, Lauren J.
Anderson, G. Darlene
Baum, David H.
Bayliss, Barbara A.
Blied, Timothy J.
Cook, D. Durand
Donnelly, Douglas R.
Flam, Joan
Gorman, Jane A.
Gradstein, Marc

Hicks, Randall B.
Hultquist, Allen C.
Lane, Karen R.
Leavitt, David Keene
Maricic, George
Michelsen, Diane
Nunez, Linda
Peck, Susan
Radis, David J.
Somit, Jed
Stocks, Janis K.
Stoddart, Ronald L.
Webster, Felice
Widelock, Marc D.
Worcester, Nanci R.

Colorado
Beltz, W. Thomas
Garvert, Melinda L.
Price, Susan

Connecticut
Stulting, Janet S.

Delaware
Meyer, Ellen S.
Tenenbaum, Joel D.

District of Columbia
McDermott, Mark T.
Scherr, Leslie
Wiernicki, Peter J.

Florida
Azulay, Daniel
Cohn, Bennett S.
McIntyre, Linda W.
Scherer, Mary Ann
Shorstein, Michael A.
Stockham, Susan L.
Swanson, Cynthia S.

Georgia
Fishbein, Rhonda
Hester, Jerrold W.
Horder, Richard A.
Steffas, Irene A.
Tanenbaum, Allan J.

Hawaii
Loomis, Laurie A.

Idaho
Hawley, John T., Jr.

Illinois
Azulay, J. Daniel
Bostick, Shelley Ballard
Cobb, Deborah Crouse
Gitlin, H. Joseph
Grammer, Susan
Hardesty, Theresa Rahe
Hirschfeld, John C.
Lifshitz, Richard A.
Morrison, Kathleen H.
Smoot, Carolyn
Weith, Glenna J.
Wildman, Sally

Indiana
Glass, Todd I.
Herrin, John Q.
Hubert, Timothy J.
Kirsh, Joel D.
Kirsh, Steven M.
Miroff, Franklin I.

Iowa
Ivers, Larry E.
Klockau, Lori L.
Randall, Ross S.

Kansas
Bauer, Martin
Bremyer-Archer, Jill
Garvert, Melinda L.
Hazlett, Allan A.
Macias, Richard A.
Vader, Joseph N.

Kentucky
Arnett, Carolyn S.
Charney, Mitchell A.
Goldman, Elisabeth
Thornton, Megan Lake
Townes, W. Waverley

Louisiana
Morris, Edith H.
Painter, David
Vargas, Noel E.

Maine
Berry, Judith M.

Maryland
Badger, Jeffrey Ewen
Berman, Jeffrey
Callahan, Ellen Ann
Davis-Loomis, Nancy
Donohue, Sara M.
Loker, Mary G.
Musgrave, Dawn Oxley
Rees, Natalie H.
Shrybman, James
Swain, Margaret E.
Thaler, Carolyn H.

Massachusetts
Crockin, Susan L.
Friedman, Herbert D.
Ginsburg, Julie E.
Greenberg, Karen K.
Kaye, Jeffrey M.
Mackin, Paula
Modica, Michele M.

Michigan
Brail, Herbert A.
Linkner, Monica Farris

Minnesota
DeSmidt, Jody O.
Gawron, Steven L.
Silberberg, Amy M.
Vincent, Judith D.
Walling, Wright S.

Mississippi
Brewer, Susan M.
Milner, Lisa B.

Missouri
Beck, Mary
Keefe, Catherine W.
Krigel, Sanford P.

Stewart, Allan F.
Wilson, Elizabeth Karsian

Nebraska
Batt, Lawrence I.
Sapp, Susan Kubert
Washburn, Michael C.

Nevada
Kunin, Israel L.
Mushkin, Rhonda

New Hampshire
Kaye, Jeffrey M.
Kuster, Ann McLane

New Jersey
Bluestein, Craig B.
Fleischner, Robin A.
Miskowski, James
Nichols, Suzanne
Sacharow, Steven B.
Solomon, Toby
Steincolor, Deborah

New Mexico
Collopy, Michael J.
Printz, Jane G.

New York
Copps, Anne Reynolds
Fleischner, Robin A.
Franklin, Gregory A.
Goldheim, Laurie B.
Goldstein, Michael S.
Herman, Flory
Kalos, Carolyn
Lewin, Stephen
Magovern, Frederick J.
Meckler, Cynthia Perla
Mesberg, Christine
Nichols, Suzanne
O'Shea, Brendan C.
Reiniger, Douglas H.
Rosenstock, Lucille
Rosin, Benjamin J.
Steincolor, Deborah
Uram, Susan W.
Zimmerman, Golda

North Carolina
Thurman, W. David
Wright, Brinton D.

Ohio
Albers, James S.
Blackmore, Margaret L.
Eisenman, Susan G.
Essig, Ellen
Franke, Carolyn Mussio
Johnson, Jerry M.
Smith, Mary E.
Swaim, James E.

Oklahoma
Bado, Barbara K.
Bado, John T.
Butler, Cynthia C.
Cubbage, William R.
Petty, Jack H.
Schaffer, Peter K.
Zimmerman, Phyllis L.

Oregon
Chally, John
Dexter, Catherine M.
Hassen, John R.
Hodgson, Sandra L.
Moffet, Susan C.
Spiegel, Laurence H.

Pennsylvania
Armhein, Richard J.
Bluestein, Craig
Bricker, Harry L., Jr.
Casey, Barbara L. Binder
Dubin, Steven G.
Fox, Debra M.
Gutterman, Tara E.
Lesko, Deborah
Leventon, Martin
Rosen, William P., III
Totaro, Samuel, Jr.

South Carolina
Bell, Richard C.
Lowndes, Thomas P.
Thompson, Fletcher D.

Thompson, James F.
Yacobi, Stephen A.

Tennessee
Buchanan, Paul M.
Coppock, S. Dawn
Tuke, Robert D.

Texas
Andrel, Vika
Bates, Gerald A.
Boydston, Karla J.
Brown, C. Harold
Clark, Mary W.
Cox, Heidi B.
Johnson, Dale R.
Lackmeyer, Michael R.
Paquet, Susan I.
Queal, Irv W.
Royall, Donald R.
Royall, Melody Brooks
Shelander, Mel W.
Yarrell, Ellen A.
Zuflacht, Linda M.

Utah
England, Les F.

Virginia
Allison, Gary B.
Ball, Teresa L.
Brust, Jennifer
Daulton, David T.
Eckman, Mark L.
Jones, Barbara C.
Klima, Robert H.
Moyer, Darlis E.
O'Brien, Rosemary G.
Phillips, Betsy H.
Phillips, Stanton E.
Poole, Rodney M.
Poster, Nancy D.
Quinn, Colleen Marea
Weinman, Ellen S.
Wexell, Richard M.

Washington
Bender, Rita L.

Demaray, Mark
Gustafson, J. Eric
Hinz, Michele Gentry
Lirhus, Albert G.

West Virginia
Barnette, David Allen

Wisconsin
Gapen, Carol M.
Hayes, Stephen W.

Newton, Judith Sperling
Schroeder, Victoria J.

Wyoming
Feeney, Peter J.

Canada
Appell, Cheryl Linda
Fahlman, Robert J.
Hodgkinson, Terry L.
Kahn, Lawrence A.

 **APPENDIX C**

Selecting a
Public Agency

our state adoption office will be very helpful in your beginning research. It can give you general information about the law and the process of adoption in your state. It can direct you to other agencies. In some states, it also places children with special needs.

Alabama Department of Human Resources
Office of Adoptions
50 N. Ripley St.
Montgomery, AL 36130
205-242-9500

Alaska Division of Family and Youth Services
Box 110630
Juneau, AK 99811
907-465-3633

Arizona Department of Economic Security
1789 West Jefferson
Phoenix, AZ 85007
602-542-2362

Arkansas Department of Human Services
Office of Adoptions
P. O. Box 1437, Slot 808
Little Rock, AR 72203
501-682-8462

California Department of Social Services
Adoption Branch
744 P St., M/S 19-69
Sacramento, CA 95814
916-445-3146

Colorado Department of Social Services
1575 Sherman St., 2nd Floor
Denver, CO 80203
303-866-3209

Connecticut Department of Children and Youth Services
Whitehall Bldg. 2, Undercliff Road
Meriden, CT 06450
203-238-6640

Delaware Division of Child Protective Services
1825 Faulkland Road
Wilmington, DE 19805
302-633-2660

District of Columbia Adoption and Placement Resources
Department of Human Services
609 H St. NE, 3rd Floor
Washington, DC 20002
202-724-8602

Florida Department of Health and Rehabilitative Services
2811 Industrial Plaza Dr.
Tallahassee, FL 32301
904-488-8262

Georgia Department of Human Resources
Division of Family and Child Services
Two Peachtree St., Ste. 313
Atlanta, GA 30309
404-657-3562

Hawaii Department of Human Services
810 Ruchards St.
Honolulu, HI 96813
808-586-5705

Idaho Department of Health and Welfare
450 W. State St.
Boise, ID 83720
208-334-5700

Illinois Department of Children and Family Services
100 W. Randolph St., 6th Floor

Chicago, IL 60612
312-814-6864

Indiana Department of Public Welfare
402 W. Washington St., W-364
Indianapolis, IN 46204
317-232-4448

Iowa Department of Human Services
Hoover State Office Bldg., 5th Floor
Des Moines, IA 50319
515-281-5358

Kansas Department of Social and Rehabilitation Services
300 SW Oakley
Topeka, KS 66606
913-296-4661

Kentucky Cabinet for Human Resources
275 E. Main St.
Frankfort, KY 40621
502-564-2136

Louisiana Department of Social Services
333 Laurel St.
Baton Rouge, LA 70821
504-342-9925

Maine Department of Human Services
221 State St.
Augusta, ME 04333
207-289-5060

Maryland Department of Human Resources
311 W. Saratoga St.
Baltimore, MD 21201
301-333-0219

Massachusetts Department of Social Services
24 Farnsworth St.
Boston, MA 02210
617-727-0900

Michigan Bureau of Family and Children Services
P.O. Box 30037
Lansing, MI 48909
517-373-3513

Minnesota Department of Human Services
Adoption Unit

444 Lafayette, 1st Floor
St. Paul, MN 55155
612-296-3740

Mississippi Department of Human Services
750 N. State St.
Jackson, MS 39202
601-359-4981

Missouri Department of Social Services
Division of Family Services
P.O. Box 88
Jefferson City, MO 65103
314-751-2502

Montana Department of Family Services
P.O. Box 8005
Helena, MT 59604
406-444-5900

Nebraska Department of Social Services
P.O. Box 95026
Lincoln, NE 68509
402-471-9331

Nevada Children and Family Services
610 Belrose St.
Las Vegas, NV 89158
702-486-5195

New Hampshire Division for Children and Youth Services
6 Hazen Dr.
Concord, NH 03301
603-271-4707

New Jersey Division of Youth and Family Services
50 E. State St., CN 717
Trenton, NJ 08625
609-984-5453

New Mexico Human Services Department
P.O. Box 2348, Rm. 225
Santa Fe, NM 87504
505-827-8417

New York State Department of Social Services
40 N. Pearl St.
Albany, NY 12243
518-474-9447

North Carolina Department of Human Resources
325 N. Salisbury St.
Raleigh, NC 27603
919-733-3801

North Dakota Department of Human Services
State Capitol
600 E. Blvd.
Bismarck, ND 58505
701-224-4805

Ohio Department of Human Services
Division of Family Services
65 E. State St., 5th Floor
Columbus, OH 43215
614-466-9274

Oklahoma Department of Human Services
P.O. Box 25352
Oklahoma City, OK 73125
405-521-4373

Oregon Department of Human Services
500 Summer St. NE
Salem, OR 97310
503-378-5093

Pennsylvania Department of Public Welfare
P.O. Box 2675
Harrisburg, PA 17105
717-787-7756

Rhode Island Department of Children and Their Families
610 Mt. Pleasant, Bldg. 5
Providence, RI 02908
401-457-4637

South Carolina Department of Social Services
P.O. Box 1520
Columbia, SC 29202
803-734-6095

South Dakota Department of Social Services
700 Governors Dr.
Pierre, SD 57501
605-773-3227

Tennessee Department of Human Services
400 Deaderick St.
Nashville, TN 37248
615-741-5935

Appendix C

Texas Department of Human Services
P.O. Box 149030, M/S W-415
Austin, TX 78714
210-450-3412

Utah Division of Family Services
120 N. 200 West, 4th Floor
Salt Lake City, UT 84103
801-538-4080

Vermont Division of Social Services
103 S. Main St.
Waterbury, VT 05671
802-241-2131

Virginia Social Services
730 E. Broad St., 2nd Floor
Richmond, VA 23219
804-692-1291

Washington Division of Children and Family Services
Mailstop 45710
Olympia, WA 98504
206-586-8200

West Virginia Department of Human Services
Capital Complex, Bldg. 6, Rm. B850
Charleston, WV 25305
304-558-7980

Wisconsin Department of Health and Social Services
P.O. Box 7851
Madison, WI 53707
608-266-0690

Wyoming Department of Health and Social Services
317 Hathaway Bldg.
Cheyenne, WY 82002
307-777-6789

 APPENDIX D

Suggested Reading for Children and International Cultural Resources

Suggested Reading for Children

Adoptive Families of America (AFA) is one of the best sources for books about adoption (see appendix A for the address). The three other best sources are:

Tapestry Books
P.O. Box 359
Ringoes, NJ 08551-0359
1-800-765-2367

EastWest Press
P.O. Box 14149
Minneapolis, MN 55414

Perspectives Press
P.O. Box 90318
Indianapolis, IN 46290

I suggest the following books to read with your child.

Angel, Ann. *Real Sister for Sure* (ages 8–12). A family adopts a biracial baby sister.

Bandish, Roslyn. *A Forever Family* (ages 5–8). A child goes from foster care to an adoptive home.

Bloom, Suzanne. *A Family for Jamie* (ages 3–8). A family is joyful at the arrival of a child.

Brodzinsky, Anne Braff. *The Mulberry Bird* (ages 4–10). A bird makes an adoption plan for her baby.

Fisher, Iris L. *Katie-Bo: An Adoption Story* (ages 3–8). A family with two biological children adopts a baby from Korea.

Fowler, Jim. *When Joel Comes Home* (ages 4–8). A friend watches the excitement of a family preparing for the arrival of a new baby.

Freudberg, Judy, and Tony Geiss. *Susan and Gordon Adopt a Baby* (ages 3–8). A Sesame Street couple adopts a baby and explains that adoption is one way to make a family.

Girard, Linda Walvoord. *Adoption Is for Always* (ages 7–11). A child works through her feelings and then starts a special family holiday to celebrate adoption day.

Girard, Linda Walvoord. *We Adopted You, Benjamin Koo* (ages 6–10). A child explores his adoption and how he handles others' attitudes.

Kasza, Keiko. *A Mother for Choco* (ages 3–8). Choco discovers the relative unimportance of physical similarity in families.

Koch, Janice. *Our Baby: A Birth and Adoption Story* (ages 2–7). The adopted child is introduced to her life story.

Koehler, Phoebe. *The Day We Met You* (younger children). This is a great arrival-day book to which you can add the details of your own experience.

Krementz, Jill. *How It Feels to Be Adopted* (ages 10 and up). Several boys and girls of various ages share what it is like to be adopted.

McNamara, Bernard and Joan. *Ordinary Miracle* (ages 3–8). Children deal with their feelings about being adopted.

Pellegrini, Nina. *Families Are Different* (ages 3–8). Korean-born children talk about being adopted and the love that binds a family together.

Rosenberg, Maxine. *Being Adopted* (ages 5–10). Children from three families talk about being adopted.

Schnitter, Jane T. *William Is My Brother* (ages 3–8). A family has both biological and adopted children.

Stein, Stephanie. *Lucy's Feet* (ages 5–10). A girl struggles with why she was adopted and her brother was not.

Stinson, Kathy. *Steven's Baseball Mitt* (ages 8–11). This book reassures children struggling with the adoption issue.

Turner, Ann. *Through Moon and Stars and Night Skies* (ages 3–8). A child journeys from a far-away country to his new family.

Waybill, Marjorie, *Chinese Eyes* (ages 4–10). A parent helps a child deal with being teased.

Wickstrom, Lois. *Oliver* (ages 3–8). Oliver imagines what life would be like if he were not adopted.

International Resources

The following sources supply international items such as books, dolls, flags, and shirts.

The Korean Connection
14 Bruce Dr.
Centereach, NY 11720-1005

The Heritage Key
6102 E. Mescal
Scottsdale, AZ 85254-5419

Notes

Chapter 2   Getting Started

1. Connie Crain and Janice Duffy, *How to Adopt a Child: A Comprehensive Guide for Prospective Parents* (Nashville: Thomas Nelson, 1994), 3.
2. Eileen M. Wirth and Joan Worden, *How to Adopt a Child from Another Country* (Nashville: Abingdon, 1993), 21.
3. Lisa Gubernick, "How Much Is That Baby in the Window?" *Forbes* (14 October 1991), 90.
4. Kay Marshall Strom and Douglas R. Donnelly, *The Complete Adoption Handbook* (Grand Rapids: Zondervan, 1992), 32.
5. Marlys Harris, "Where Have All the Babies Gone?" *Money Magazine* (December 1988), 166.
6. Ibid., 168.
7. Lewis Lord, "Desperately Seeking Baby," *U.S. News and World Report* (5 October 1987), 58.

Chapter 3   Adoption Law

1. Nancy Thalia Reynolds, *Adopting Your Child* (North Vancouver, B.C., Canada: Self-Counsel Press, 1994), 150.
2. Michael R. Sullivan, *Adopt the Baby You Want* (New York: Simon and Schuster, 1990), 59.
3. Randall B. Hicks, *Adopting in America* (Sun City, Calif.: Wordslinger Press, 1995), 101–7.

Chapter 4   Why Adopt?

1. Wirth and Worden, *How to Adopt a Child from Another Country*, 16.
2. Strom and Donnelly, *The Complete Adoption Handbook*, 28.
3. Lois Gilman, *The Adoption Resource Book* (New York: HarperCollins, 1992), 15–16.

4. Sherry Bunin, "Up with Adoption," *Parents* (January 1990), 78.

5. "Adoption or Maladoption?" *Society* (March/April 1993), 2.

6. Jayne E. Schooler, *The Whole Life Adoption Book* (Colorado Springs: Pinon Press, 1994), 15.

7. Ibid., 73.

8. Douglas R. Donnelly, "A Guide to Adoption," (Colorado Springs: Focus on the Family, 1991), 20.

9. Bruce Rappaport, *The Open Adoption Book* (New York: Macmillan, 1992), 181.

10. Cheryl Sacra, "Adopted Joy," *Health* (May 1991), 17.

11. Elaine Walker, *Loving Journeys Guide to Adoption* (Peterborough, N.H.: Loving Journeys, 1992), 47.

12. "Adoption: A Guide for Parents" (Birmingham, Ala.: The American Fertility Society), 8.

Chapter 5   Adopting after Infertility

1. Patricia Irwin Johnston, *Adopting after Infertility* (Indianapolis: Perspectives Press, 1992), 48.

2. Jill Smolowe, "The Pain of Infertility," *Adoptive Families* (January/February 1995), 20.

3. Jill Baughan, *A Hope Deferred: A Couple's Guide to Coping with Infertility* (Portland, Ore.: Multnomah, 1989), 15.

4. Walker, *Loving Journeys*, 45.

5. Ibid., 45.

Chapter 6   Can I Adopt the Child I Want?

1. Marianne Takas, *To Love a Child* (Reading, Mass.: Addison-Wesley, 1992), 4.

2. Ibid., 5.

3. Strom and Donnelly, *The Complete Adoption Handbook*, 67.

4. Walker, *Loving Journeys*, 35.

5. The classic work on this type of adoption is Claudia L. Jewett, *Adopting the Older Child* (Harvard, Mass.: Harvard Common Press, 1978). It covers in depth the decision to adopt an older child, how to prepare the child, and how to prepare yourselves. It also provides lots of further information and encouragement.

6. Wirth and Worden, *How to Adopt a Child from Another Country*, 137.

7. Walker, *Loving Journeys*, 35.

8. Jill Smolowe, "Adoption in Black and White," *Time* (14 August 1995), 50.

9. "Transracial and Transcultural Adoption" (Rockville, Md.: The National Adoption Information Clearinghouse).

10. Bill Holton, "Loving Elizabeth," *Family Circle* (19 October 1995), 94.

11. Wirth and Worden, *How to Adopt a Child from Another Country,* 133.

12. Walker, *Loving Journeys,* 37.

13. *AFA's Guide to Adoption* (Minneapolis: Adoptive Families of America), 15.

14. Strom and Donnelly, *The Complete Adoption Handbook,* 104.

Chapter 7   An Adoption Overview

1. Hicks, *Adopting in America,* 12.

2. Reynolds, *Adopting Your Child,* 124.

3. Wirth and Worden, *How to Adopt a Child from Another Country,* 123.

4. Joan D. Ramos, "The Tough Ethical Issues of International Adoption," *OURS* (January/February 1994), 14.

5. Gilman, *The Adoption Resource Book,* 167.

6. Ramos, "The Tough Ethical Issues of International Adoption," 14.

7. Wirth and Worden, *How to Adopt a Child from Another Country,* 65.

8. Reynolds, *Adopting Your Child,* 144.

9. Gilman, *The Adoption Resource Book,* 77.

10. Nancy Gibbs, "The Baby Chase," *Time* (9 October 1989), 89.

11. Stanley B. Michelman and Meg Schneider, *The Private Adoption Handbook* (New York: Dell, 1988), 13. A couple from Chicago whom I interviewed for this book has used an advertising method to locate their son. They, along with many other couples who have realized their dreams of becoming a family, strongly recommend this book. It is a comprehensive guide to independent adoption covering everything from how to write a newspaper ad to how to screen calls. Make this the next book on your reading list if you are interested in independent adoption.

12. Arty Elgart, *Golden Cradle: How the Adoption Establishment Works and How to Make It Work for You* (New York: Citadel Press, 1991), 25–26.

13. Kathleen Cushman, "Advertising for Babies," *Woman's Day* (5 November 1991), 52.

14. Jerry Ann Jenista, "Financing an Adoption," *OURS* (November/December 1990), 24.

15. Wirth and Worden, *How to Adopt a Child from Another Country,* 47.

Chapter 8   The Home Study

1. Katherine Davis Fishman, "Problem Adoptions," *Atlantic Monthly* (September 1992), 37.

2. Elizabeth Bartholet, *Family Bonds: Adoption and the Politics of Parenting* (New York: Houghton Mifflin, 1993), 46.

3. Wirth and Worden, *How to Adopt a Child from Another Country,* 20.

4. Gilman, *The Adoption Resource Book*, 56.

5. Reynolds, *Adopting Your Child*, 75.

Chapter 9   The Waiting Game

1. Laura Jordan, "Becoming an Adoptive Family," *Parents* (August 1995), 129.

2. Wirth and Worden, *How to Adopt a Child from Another Country*, 56.

3. Ibid., 51.

4. Jordan, "Becoming an Adoptive Family," 129.

5. Elgart, *Golden Cradle*, 189.

6. Gilman, *The Adoption Resource Book*, 219.

7. Bonnie Olson and Rita Emmenegger, "Learning the Basics," *OURS* (May/June 1994), 24–25.

8. Baughan, *A Hope Deferred*, 168.

9. James L. Moline, "Pampering Your Partner while You Wait to Adopt," *OURS* (January/February 1994), 22.

10. Elgart, *Golden Cradle*, 188.

11. Moline, "Pampering Your Partner," 22.

12. Patricia Irwin Johnston, "Getting Friends and Family Excited about Adoption," *Adoptive Families* (July/August 1994), 26–27.

13. Wirth and Worden, *How to Adopt a Child from Another Country*, 84.

14. Walker, *Loving Journeys*, 61.

15. Deborah McCurdy, "Choosing a Name for Your Foreign-Born Child," *Roots and Wings* (Spring 1995), 21.

16. Terra Trevor, "The Ups and Downs of Waiting," *Adoptive Families* (July/August 1994), 35.

17. Angela Elwell Hunt, *The Adoption Option* (Wheaton: Victor Books, 1989), 71.

Chapter 10   Your Child Arrives

1. Gilman, *The Adoption Resource Book*, 255.

2. Ibid., 252.

3. Stephanie Siegel, *Parenting Your Adopted Child* (New York: Prentice Hall, 1989), 16–17.

4. Holly van Gulden and Lisa Bartels-Rabb, *Real Parents, Real Children* (New York: Crossroad, 1995), 76.

5. Schooler, *The Whole Life Adoption Book*, 81.

6. van Gulden and Bartels-Rabb, *Real Parents, Real Children*, 17.

7. Schooler, *The Whole Life Adoption Book*, 82.

8. Ibid., 86.

9. Dorothy W. Smith and Laurie Nehls Sherwen, *Mothers and Their Adopted Children: The Bonding Process* (New York: Tiresias Press, 1988), 60–61.

10. Lois Melina, *Making Sense of Adoption* (New York: Harper and Row, 1989), 145.

Chapter 11 Talking about Adoption

1. Laura Giardina, "I Carried You in My Heart," *Children Today* (September/October 1990), 6.

2. Charlene Canape, *Adoption: Parenthood without Pregnancy* (New York: Henry Holt, 1986), 131–32.

3. Schooler, *The Whole Life Adoption Book,* 120–21.

4. Giardina, "I Carried You in My Heart," 7.

5. Melina, *Making Sense of Adoption,* 22–23.

6. Strom and Donnelly, *The Complete Adoption Handbook,* 139.

7. Kathryn Creedy, "When Kids Ask about Adoption," *Adoptive Families* (July/August 1994), 9.

8. Melina, *Making Sense of Adoption,* 62.

9. Canape, *Adoption,* 133.

10. Melina, *Making Sense of Adoption,* 84.

11. Ibid., 137.

12. Lois Melina, *Raising Adopted Children* (New York: Harper and Row, 1986), 67.

13. Gilman, *The Adoption Resource Book,* 286.

14. Schooler, *The Whole Life Adoption Book,* 141.

15. van Gulden and Bartels-Rabb, *Real Parents, Real Children,* 37.

16. Melina, *Making Sense of Adoption,* 165.

17. Wirth and Worden, *How to Adopt a Child from Another Country,* 100.

18. Melina, *Making Sense of Adoption,* 211.

19. Strom and Donnelly, *The Complete Adoption Handbook,* 147, 149.

20. Canape, *Adoption,* 139.

21. Schooler, *The Whole Life Adoption Book,* 206–7.

22. Troy Segal, "When Adoptees Want to Dig Up Their Roots," *Business Week* (14 October 1991), 122.

23. Hunt, *The Adoption Option,* 129.

24. Siegel, *Parenting Your Adopted Child,* 156–57.

25. Gilman, *The Adoption Resource Book,* 305.

26. Schooler, *The Whole Life Adoption Book,* 208.

27. Siegel, *Parenting Your Adopted Child,* 155.

28. Charmainse Crouse Yoest, "The Lucky Ones," *Children Today* (November/December 1990), 12.

29. Bruce Bower, "Adapting to Adoption," *Science News* (13 August 1994), 104.

30. Yoest, "The Lucky Ones," 13.

31. Strom and Donnelly, *The Complete Adoption Handbook,* 163–64.

32. Melina, *Making Sense of Adoption,* 59.

33. Melina, *Raising Adopted Children,* 66–67.

Chapter 12 Adoption and Others

1. Melina, *Making Sense of Adoption,* 40.

2. Cheri Register, "Are White People Colorless?" *OURS* (January/February 1994), 32.

3. Melina, *Raising Adopted Children,* 78–79.

4. Rita Laws, "Four Adoption Terms Defined," *OURS* (May/June 1986), 32.

Chapter 13   Open versus Closed Adoption

1. Strom and Donnelly, *The Complete Adoption Handbook,* 49.

2. Ruth McRoy, Harold Grotevant, and Susan Ayers-Lopez, "Open Adoption," *Adoptive Families* (January/February 1995), 16.

3. Gilman, *The Adoption Resource Book,* 102.

4. Ibid., 118.

5. Lois Melina and Sharon Kaplan-Roszia, *The Open Adoption Experience* (New York: HarperCollins, 1993), 40.

6. Sullivan, *Adopt the Baby You Want,* 104.

7. Strom and Donnelly, *The Complete Adoption Handbook,* 49.

8. Lincoln Caplan, "An Open Adoption," *The New Yorker* (28 May 1990), 77–78.

9. Ibid., 78.

10. An excellent resource on open adoption is Melina and Kaplan-Roszia, *The Open Adoption Experience.*

Chapter 14   The Future

1. Canape, *Adoption,* 146.

2. Richard Jerome, "The Homecoming," *People Weekly* (29 May 1995), 40.

3. Michelle Ingrassia, "Ordered to Surrender," *Newsweek* (6 February 1995), 45.

4. Sullivan, *Adopt the Baby You Want,* 213–19.

5. Melina, *Making Sense of Adoption,* 4–7.

Chapter 15   God's Adopted Children

1. Wirth and Worden, *How to Adopt a Child from Another Country,* 111.

Christine Moriarty Field, former criminal prosecutor and private attorney, is now a stay-at-home mom and author of *Coming Home to Raise Your Children* (Revell, 1995). She and her husband have three daughters and are in the process of adopting a fourth child. They live in Wheaton, Illinois.